ONLY IN THE CRUCIFIED GOD

Questions and Answers on Faith, Hope and Love

BY

SEAN LOONE

ONLY IN THE CRUCIFIED GOD

FRANCIS,

MAY GOD BLESS YOU
NOW AND ALWAYS.

DEACON SEAN

OCTOBER 2020

*'As it is, these three remain, faith, hope
and love, the three of them; and the
greatest of these is love.'*

(1 Corinthians 13:13)

Saint Paul

This book is dedicated to all those who walk or who have walked in darkness

'The people that walked in darkness have seen a great light; on the inhabitants of a country in shadow dark as death, light has blazed forth'

(Isaiah 9:1)

CONTENTS

CONTENTS

FOREWARD

This is a book written for people living in darkness and who need somewhere to turn. From suffering, pain, anxiety, stress, depression and even death emerges the light of God's love, always present and never absent. However, where is this God? What, in fact, is this God like? Does this God love everyone? What is faith? Where was this God when I needed him most? If this God came to change everything, why is everything still the same? All these questions and more are answered in the pages of this book. Yet it is not the author who provides the answers but God himself through His written word, the Bible. Using scripture as God's love letter to the human race, the pages of this book reveal a God who is willing to do anything, even die a brutal and agonising death on a cross, to reveal the full depth of his love for all people. This is the Crucified God and only in Him are all the answers to all of our questions, ultimately to be found. So bring with you your own experiences of life, whether they are good or bad and immerse them in the pages of this book. You might just be surprised at what happens when you arrive at the end to find out that, in fact, it is only the beginning. *There is one thing, however, that I want to make abundantly clear right from the start and that is all profit from the sale of this book, whether they be physical or digital, will be donated to CAFOD – The Catholic Association For Overseas Development. CAFOD is a charity dedicated to helping and supporting some of the poorest and most deprived people on the planet. More information about CAFOD can be found on the website: CAFOD.org.uk. The pages of this book often explore the darkness people experience in life. Christianity is nothing less than an invitation by the 'Crucified God' to bring the light of his love to those who know only pain and suffering.*

INTRODUCTION

If you are taking the time to read this book, that is to say some of it or all of it, then I would ask you to do one thing, bring your own experiences of life with you and immerse them in every page. To this end, never, ever underestimate the importance of what you have been through in life whether that has been good or bad. You see what you will find, I hope, in the pages of this book are questions people have asked me about life, faith and their own experiences. In response what I have tried to do guided by the grace of the Holy Spirit, is to help people find the answers for themselves. For me only God can meet our deepest needs and desires and only God, therefore, can answer that which we yearn for most. Now, I will say this time and time again throughout the pages of this book, God is closer to use than we could ever imagine, just waiting for us, like a father standing on a hilltop waiting for his wayward son to return home. If then, we are brave enough to look deep into our own hearts, embrace our own experiences and be open to God, something wonderful happens. However, do not take my word for it, just give it a go for yourself. At the very least then I would ask you to approach this book with an open mind, read as much, or as little as you like and then come to your own conclusions. The book is divided into chapters each having its own question and answer. You can read the chapters in any order, simply choose a question, which interests you, the most, read my proposed answer and then move on stopping whenever and wherever you like. If you can though, do try to make it through to the end and then just see what happens. Do not be afraid, however, to put the book to one side from time to time to give yourself the opportunity to think things through. Equally, have a pencil in your hand, underline things you find of interest and jot your own questions in the margin, after all this is a book that is meant to be used!

I now want to say something about why I have chosen the title, *'Only in the Crucified God.'* My home parish is called Our Lady of the Wayside and it can be found in Shirley in the West Midlands. It is a modern church built in 1965 as part of the reform instituted by the Second Vatican Council. As you enter the building you find yourself in a modern narthex with a baptistery, complete with running water, on your right hand side and a side chapel on your left. Just as you pass the side chapel, again on your left, before you pass through a set of glass doors leading into the main body of the church you will find something quite remarkable, though easily missed. For built into the brick wall is an image of the Crucified Christ. It is life sized and hugely dramatic as his crucified body learns forward from the cross with his long hair covering his tortured face. What made the point for me though is the fact that you have to pass this image to actually get into the church. Once inside you will be confronted by another impressive site, standing behind the altar and raised up for all to see is a statue of the risen Jesus, complete with the wounds from his crucifixion, representing his resurrection and therefore his victory over,

Satan, sin and death. What struck me at this point, as I reflected on what I was seeing, is that before we reach the resurrection, the high point of our faith, we have to pass through the crucifixion. And passing that image of the crucified Jesus on the way into church makes that very point. Jesus came for us and revealed the overwhelming nature of God's love for us by dying on the cross, which is the very essence of what was being said to me as I stared at this brutal image serving to reveal the true nature and being of God. Could it not be that our lives are destined to follow this pattern too? Then I remembered something that Jesus said, *'Anyone who wants to be a follower of mine must renounce self and take up the cross and follow me. For whoever, wants to save his life will lose it; but whoever loses his life for me sake will find it.'* (Matthew 16:24-25) Suddenly everything for me then fell into place and I knew exactly why I had to call this book, *'Only in the Crucified God.'* Firstly, as I have already said the crucifixion reveals the depth of God's love for us through his pain and his suffering. Secondly, the truth is that in life all of us sooner or later suffer and yet we never do so alone because God is always with us. (Matthew 28:20) This is because God's life is so intimately bound up with ours that it is impossible to separate the two. In this way, it could be said, that all suffering can be seen as nothing less than a participation in the suffering of God. This is why our experiences in life are so important because all of them are potential encounters with God if, only, we have the eyes of faith to see them, to embrace them and believe them. This is called the theology of experience and is a way of understanding God, which can lead to the transformation of our lives and indeed everything. But if this is ever going to happen we have to change first.

Finally, although people have asked me all the questions in this book I have tried, as far as possible, to allow God to answer each and every single one of them. To achieve this I have used God's word, the Bible, to substantiate any claims I have made. Equally I have not been afraid to use my own personal experiences of life to illustrate my central theme in the book that it is in them we encounter the living God. I have set these words down, guided by God's grace, for anybody who has found themselves in turmoil and has not known where to turn. For me all the answers, to our deepest questions, are to be found, ultimately, in the *'Crucified God,'* and it is to him that every single word in this book points.

'The thought of God's mercy in the cross of Christ is the

only thing that sustains me'

Padre Pio

CHAPTER ONE

'Why?'

'If anyone wants to be a follower of mine, let him renounce himself and take up his cross and follow me' (Matthew 16:24)

The first question in this book I ask of myself, *'Why are you writing it?'* Then I go on to ask, *'Who are you writing it for?'* These are questions I feel I must ask and then answer if I am to prepare you, the reader, for what is to follow. You may, of course, have questions of your own such as, *'Why am I reading this book?'* or *'What do I hope to get out of it?'* but, if I may, I will, at least for now leave answers to questions such as these up to you.

She

She came from a family of seven with two sisters and four brothers, living on a small farm in county Mayo in the West of Ireland. The house was one of those whitewashed, almost picture-postcard type cottages, that you often see on biscuit tins and the like. Life, however, was far from romantic living in such a harsh environment. There was no electricity and no gas with the sole source of cooking and heating being the peat-fuelled fire, which was the centre of the home. There was one main living space, which contained a table and a small alcove separated from the rest of the room by a curtain, this served as her parent's bedroom, providing some degree of privacy. The children, on the other hand, often slept in a single room with the boys and the girls in two separate beds. Life on the farm was harsh with early morning starts, long walks to school and all the necessary chores that needed to be completed if they were ever going to survive, especially the long cold winters. At school she learned to read, write and do basic mathematics but that was about it. The driving force was to earn your keep as soon as possible the only problem being that there were no jobs, outside the farm, for miles around. Eventually it became impossible for the family to exist and support nine individuals, so with no employment in the local area one by one her sisters and brothers looked across the water to England for a better life.

Eventually this was where she gazed too and with high expectations of a new and better life she set off for the industrial city of Birmingham where employment was more or less guaranteed. How different life must have looked in this new cosmopolitan city with its dance halls, cinemas and well-dressed locals. With the little money she had managed to save she found a small room to rent and work in a nearby factory. Now, perhaps for the first time in her life, she could actually live in a comfortable way. Yet she never forgot where she came from and always sent money back to the old country for her parents to help them stave off the harsh realities of life on the farm. So with money in her pocket and a smile on her face she could at last afford to buy herself the odd treat, perhaps a handbag or a pair of earrings, a new skirt or a cardigan and even a night out on the town. For the most part she stuck with those she knew which meant the other Irish immigrants who flooded the inner parts of Birmingham making the slum areas their own, after all who else would want to live there? Huge crowds would gather after mass on a Sunday to catch up on life back at home and to feel part of something bigger than themselves. She was making a new life for herself and it must have felt good.

Then one day she met somebody and they fell in love. He received instructions in the Catholic faith and they were married soon after. They say that love is blind but I cannot help but wonder did she really know what she was letting herself in for? The man she married was a veteran of the Second World War and in ways few of us can ever begin to imagine was broken by his experiences there. I have no doubt that, at first, they were happy and not long after they were married they had their first child a son, followed by a daughter then sadly a miscarriage. You see her husband was a heavy drinker possibly his way of coping and breaking down the memories that followed him home from the war. But alcohol brings with it much more than just the drink. There were those times when, in the morning, after a heaving drinking session the night before he simply could not get up to go to work the next day. Who would put food on the table and clothes on the children's' backs then? Then came the gambling! Again was it to forget? Was it for the thrill? Or was it just a distraction from what life had become? Perhaps it was all these things but whatever the truth was things began to spiral out of control. There were arguments, fights, late nights, debt, times when he would not come home at all or even not be seen for days, what was she to do now?

The most precious thing in life to her was her children and she would do whatever it took to provide for them. So now she was forced to do what she had always done, work. Sometimes it was cleaning, sometimes it was in a factory, sometimes it was both but day in and day out she would work and work and work, almost to the point of physical and mental exhaustion. Her sole motivation was to provide for her two children. She would be the one to make sure that they had the right school uniform. She would be the one to make sure that they were fed and nourished. She would be the one to make sure that life for them would be as normal as it could be when in reality it was far from that. Gone now were the earrings, handbags and the odd treat, instead the only luxury she allowed herself was cigarettes and these were eventually to lead to her death.

Life for her then was not easy, it never had been and it never would be again, that was just the way it was. The children struggled. The boy became pasty looking and seriously under weight to the point that the doctors had to send him for sunray treatment. There he would sit, bare-chested, with goggles on in front of a sunray lamp along with several other boys in an attempt to reverse a serious deficiency in vitamin D. They found it hard to make progress at school because of the late nights they had to endure along with the arguments, fights and disagreements over money. Sometimes the rent failed to be paid or they fell into arrears over something they had been forced to buy on credit. There were no holidays, no central heating, no telephone, no car, no luxuries just existence if you could call it that. And all the while she continued to work.

Certain things in life you can only put up with for so long until in the end they grind you down. Day by day, month-by-month, year-by-year hoping that things would improve, maybe get better even but they rarely do. In the end life just beats you. You run out of energy. It happens slowly but you start to get weak. In the past you fell down but you knew, she knew, you had to get up again there was no other option but one day you fall and you just cannot get back up. Do not get me wrong, you want to but your strength has gone, it has been consumed by life. Now the weight is just too heavy to bear anymore. You see, her children had grown up, now they were standing on their own two feet, her job was complete and it was time to let go. At first it was a stroke, which confined her to bed, then the weakness and the cruelty of life just simply overwhelmed her. Her son took the hand she could no long use and rubbed it gently down the side of his face, she smiled and one tear left the corner of her eye and rolled gently down her cheek. The lines on her face told her story but only he could read it. It was time to let go now, her strength was gone, and she had nothing more to give. She closed her eyes for the last time and would never open them again in this life. Now it was the turn of her son to wipe the tears away from his face but he knew her story and one day, when the time was right, he would tell it.

I have just told you the story of my own Mother who loved both my sister and myself fiercely, absolutely and completely. She loved until she had, literally, nothing else left to give. It was as if she actually gave up her own life so that we could have one. Imagine that, someone whose love was so total, so committed and so uncompromising that it motivated everything she did. So we come to that question, '*Why?*' Why have I told you this story? Well I have told you, the reader, this story so that anyone who reads it, who might be going through those dark experiences of life might know and believe that no matter how dark the night might be there is always light and therefore hope. I did not realise it at the time but it was to come to me clearly later that through the love of my own mother I was, in fact, experiencing nothing less than the love of God. This was to be my light in the darkness and when my eyes were finally opened I began to see a reality that had been there all along, the *'Crucified God.'*

I remember once looking at my Mum's hands covered in blue sticking plasters and wondering what that was all about. Later I was to learn that working in poor lighting in a factory and suffering from weak eyesight her fingers were often caught by the sharp tools on the machines she operated. Those hands were often dirty, covered in grease and smelling of detergent but they were the hands of love. With those hands she would work and slave day and night never stopping, always on the go. Sometimes there were two jobs one early in the morning the other late in the evening; she even worked nights for a while. She wrote the story of her life on those hands and one day I found myself able to read it. I say this because eventually I came across another pair of hands equally dirty and covered in small cuts from the splinters of wood he handled. There was dirt beneath the fingernails callouses on the thumbs and if you looked closely enough deep wounds in the wrists. These also were the hands of love and the price they paid was terrible. Yet I discovered a *'treasure hidden in a field'* when I began to understand something of this *'Crucified God'* and this is what I want to offer you, the reader, as we begin this journey together. For it is in the experience of our own lives that we are to discover the reality of God. As a result, I would urge you, to treasure your own experiences of life no matter how dark they might be and to discover in them the true nature and being of God. For he is the one who comes for you, he is the one who lives those experiences with you, he is the one who is closer to you and loves you more than you could ever imagine and he is the one who will never, ever be separated from you, not even in death. He is the one who walks out of the darkness and offers us those broken and crucified hands, he is the one who revealed himself to us as the God who is prepared to do anything, anything at all for us, for one reason and one reason only, love. I was not taught this from any theology book or even the church but from my own Mother whose life made God's love a living reality for me. When my Mum died, therefore, there was one reading from the New Testament I knew I had to have at her funeral. It comes from Saint Paul's letter to the Romans and it was written towards the end of his life. Paul, you see, had suffered greatly because of his faith in Jesus Christ. He had been rejected by his own people, mocked, stoned, flogged, driven out of a number of towns and cities, imprisoned and even shipwrecked on more than one occasion. Eventually he was placed under house arrest before being executed two years later. However, despite all of this Paul was still able to write these remarkable words,

'For I am certain of this that neither death nor life, no angel, no prince, nothing that exists, nothing still to come, not any power, or height or depth, nor any created thing will ever come between us and the love of God made visible in Christ Jesus our Lord.' (Romans 8: 38-39)

For me there is real power in these words, *'For I am certain that …….. nothing will be able to separate us from the love of God made visible in Christ Jesus our Lord.'* The first time I heard them they spoke directly to me, all those things I had gone through, experienced and witnessed, God had been there all along, suffering them with me but at the same time never withdrawing his love. The late nights, the bad language, the alcohol, the lack of food, money, clothing, the poor housing, the gambling, all those evenings waiting outside a pub, the arguments, the cruelty, the desperation, the list is endless but there is another constant and that is the love of the *'Crucified God.'*

Through all those times I never, ever, once remember my Mum not being there for me when I needed it. In the same way as later I became familiar with the scriptures I began to understand how the *'Crucified God,'* also never seemed to turn his back on anyone in need. Then one day when I was about sixteen I remember suffering from terrible toothache. I was, in fact, in agony and I am not exaggerating. The dentist was not a place I was familiar with so I turned up at a local surgery expecting help, relief or at least some kind of advice. Instead without a word of sympathy, help or support I was just turned away. In other words they turned their backs on me. I resolved that day that in my life I would never, if at all possible, turn my back on anyone who asked me for help. In the end I found my way to a local authority school dentist who went out of their way to help me. At this point I could not help but smile as I remembered fond memories of my Mum always giving to anyone who asked of her, including those begging in the street. She never turned her back on anyone. This is how life should be, I remember thinking. So now my first task is almost complete. I asked myself, *'Why are you writing this book?'* And the answer is to help anybody who needs it, in so far as the words and experiences I offer here are my humble attempt to reveal something of the nature and being of the *'Crucified God,'* and that takes me to the next question.

'Why the Crucified God?'

In his letter to the Philippians Saint Paul says something quite remarkable about God and his son Jesus, *'His state was divine, yet he did not cling to his equality with God but emptied himself to assume the condition of a slave.'* (Philippians 2: 6-7) I shall refer to this passage again later in the book but for now I will make the point about how, once again, these words spoke directly to me out of my own experiences of life. The extract is referring to Jesus and states quite clearly from the beginning that he is God (divine). However, it then goes on to say how he gave this divinity up, emptying himself to become a slave. What we are seeing here is a God who comes to search for us, a God who comes to find us and a God who is willing to do anything for us. In the Roman Catholic Church on the final Sunday of the liturgical year, the one before Advent, we celebrate 'Christ the King.' Here we focus our attention on Jesus, whose throne is a cross, whose crown is one made up of thorns and whose body is broken, battered and bruised. This is the *'Crucified God.'* This is the one who in coming to find us suffers the most terrible and humiliating death possible but he does so willingly out of love. In that figure on the cross the values of the world are transformed and turned upside down. Power is found in weakness, hope is found in despair, light is found in darkness and life is found in death. Little wonder then that this is the God who I believe spoke directly to me out of my own life experience. In all honesty this is the only God I could ever believe in or place all my faith, hope and trust in, for this is the God who has experienced every moment of my own darkness with me. This is the God who, therefore, has credibility because he can literally say, I know for *'I am with you always.'* (Matthew 28: 20)

At this point I am going to pause a little bit because I feel the need to drill down deeper into understanding why I have called this book, *'Only in the Crucified God.'* Crucifixion was a way of executing prisoners found in ancient Rome. It had been developed over many years, through trial and error, to maximise pain, suffering and humiliation for the prisoner. Its aim was to prolong death for as long as possible both to make the victim suffer but also to serve as an example for anyone who potentially was thinking of threatening Rome and its empire. We know that the Romans crucified thousands of people but strangely few of their names have been preserved. This is because the vast majority of them were slaves, nothings and nobodies in the eyes of the empire. These were people to be dealt with and disposed of and Jesus fell into this category. We also know that Jesus was scourged first, the normal prelude to crucifixion. (Matthew 27:26) Here he would have been repeatedly beaten with a *'flagrum'* a wooden stick to which were attached strips of leather containing sharpened pieces of metal or bone. At this point he would have struggled to stand up because of the blood loss and the fact that he had been on trial for most of the previous night and was therefore weak. Still he was now stripped and humiliated by the Roman soldiers. They made him a crown of thorns, placed a scarlet cloak about him and put a reed into his right hand as they bowed before him and said, *'Hail King of the Jews.'* (Matthew 27-30). Finally, they spat at him and struck him over the head with the reed. (Matthew 27:31) In the end they led him away to be crucified. By now Jesus was too weak to carry his own cross so a man was taken from the crowd called Simon of Cyrene to bare this burden for him. Eventually they came to a place called the skull or Golgotha. (Matthew 27:32-33) It is important to realise at this point that his closest followers, the disciples, abandoned him and that the place he was to be executed at was outside the holy city of Jerusalem. In this way he is rejected by everyone including the religious leaders of the day who in doing so, perhaps thought, that God was also abandoning him.

The full horrific details of crucifixion are never described in the gospels but the cruel, cold, efficiency of the soldiers are clear to see. Nails through the wrists, which are strong enough to hold the body up followed by nails through the feet makes movement, for the prisoner, almost impossible. The victim would also have been crucified naked in order to maximise humiliation. The crowd now jeered and mocked him, *'He saved others; he cannot save himself.'* (Matthew 27:42) Finally, when the pain becomes unbearable Jesus cries out, *'My God, My God, why have you forsaken me?'* (Matthew 27: 46) Too poor to own a tomb he is buried in one provided by an admirer called Joseph of Arimathea. (Matthew 27: 57-61) Yet for the Christian this is God we are talking about and describing. A God who willingly subjected himself to all of this for one reason and one reason only, love. There have been many things written about the crucifixion but for me the one thing that speaks most powerfully about what God is really like is to be found here. I reflected earlier on, in this chapter, how Roman Catholics every year celebrate 'Christ the King,' at the end of the liturgical year. Well this is our king. Equally on Good Friday the Church holds up, before the faithful people of God, the image of Christ crucified as a reminder of the depth of God's love and the length he is prepared to go to reveal the full extent of his love for us. For me this is the only way God can have any credibility at all. To become one with us, to suffer with us and to constantly be with us for no other reason than he loves us. I caught a glimpse of that love in the life of my own Mother and it changed my life forever. It is no coincidence that when Jesus was raised from the dead the wounds of his crucifixion, though transformed, remained with him. (John 20: 24-29) In the same way the wounds of our own lives although they stay with us are transformed by the love of his grace. This is, in essence, the very reason how I am able both to write this chapter and indeed this whole book.

If you have made it this far and would like to explore what comes next and I hope you do. Then there is a wonderful invitation in John's Gospel. It comes right at the beginning when Jesus calls his first disciples. He simply says to them, *'Come and see,'* (John 1: 39) and their lives would never be the same again. That now becomes my invitation to you, the reader, as you approach what lies ahead, simply *'Come and see.'* Choose any chapter you like, read it and see what happens and leave the rest up to his grace, which comes to us from the loving arms of the *'Crucified God.'*

CHAPTER TWO

'Where is God?

'For indeed, the Kingdom of God is within you.' (Luke 17:21)

In many ways this is the question I am most often asked, *'Where is God?'* It raises huge issues and I am not sure what people expect when it comes to an answer. Are people looking to be told something? If so would any answer I come up with ever satisfy them? On the other hand are people asking to be shown the way, to be pointed in the right direction, you might say? Or are people asking for an experience, one that will prove, at least for them, the existence of God?

The way I am going to answer this question will require you, the reader, to do something but only if you want to. I will offer an invitation, in the same way that God constantly invites us to know him and my answer will,

I hope, be part of this process. However, I will also ask you to give up some time, to put some effort in, as it were, to help you understand the answer to the question, which I am offering. If you do that then you might be surprised at the answer to the question, *'Where is God?'*

The starting point actually lies within us. Look at what Jesus said in the Gospel of Luke, *'For indeed, the Kingdom of God is within you.'* (Luke 17:21) Have you ever thought about that? That the very first place to start looking for God is within your own self? I remember once reading something about the scientist Albert Einstein. One of his students once asked him what they might do for their doctoral thesis and to the student's great surprise Einstein answered by saying *'prayer.'* Humanity, he went on to explain, has spent so much time studying the universe outside of ourselves that we have neglected that which lies within. In the Gospel of Matthew Jesus says, *'the kingdom of heaven is like treasure hidden in a field which someone has found; he hides it again, goes off happy, sells everything he owns and buys the field.'* (Matthew 13:44) Imagine then, if that treasure Jesus is talking about is within you, just waiting to be discovered. Jesus goes on to say, *'Again, the kingdom of heaven is like a merchant looking for fine pearls; when he finds one of great value he goes and sells everything he owns and buys it.'* (Luke 13: 45-46) What if the pearl of great value has been within you all along but you have just never known it?

If we are to make the journey within then we have to do something and I will explain what that might be in a moment. Firstly, though we need to understand how important prayer was to Jesus. There are many examples to be found in the Bible describing Jesus at prayer, here are some of them,'

'Now when all the people were baptized, and when Jesus also had been baptized and was praying, the heaven was opened.' (Luke 3:21)

'Once when Jesus was praying alone, with only the disciples near him, he asked them, "Who do the crowds say that I am?" (Luke 9:18)

'But I have prayed for you that your own faith may not fail; and you, when once you have turned back, strengthen your brothers." (Luke 22:32)

'Now during those days he went out to the mountain to pray; and he spent the night in prayer to God.' (Luke 6:12)

'But he would withdraw to deserted places and pray.' (Luke 5:16)

'In the morning, while it was still very dark, he got up and went out to a deserted place, and there he prayed.' (Mark 1:35)

'They went to a place called Gethsemane; and he said to his disciples, "Sit here while I pray." He took with him Peter and James and John, and began to be distressed and agitated. And he said to them, "I am deeply grieved, even to death; remain here, and keep awake." And going a little farther, he threw himself on the ground and prayed that, if it were

possible, the hour might pass from him.' (Mark 14: 32-35)

'Then little children were being brought to him in order that he might lay his hands on them and pray.' (Matthew 19:13)

'And after he had dismissed the crowds, he went up the mountain by himself to pray. When evening came, he was there alone.' (Matthew 14:23)

'But even now I know that God will give you whatever you ask of him.' (John11: 22)

'I ask not only on behalf of these, but also on behalf of those who will believe in me through their word.' (John 17:20)

'And I will ask the Father, and he will give you another Advocate, to be with you forever.' (John 14:16)

I have provided a number of references from the Bible, above, to highlight how important prayer was to Jesus. We can only assume that he both wanted and needed to spend time, alone, with his Father. In truth, however, we do not know the content, for the most, of this private prayer time. What we do know though is that the disciples, perhaps inspired by

Jesus, asked him how to pray and this is what he said,

> *'Our Father in heaven,*
> *hallowed be your name.*
> *Your kingdom come.*
> *Your will be done,*
> *on earth as it is in heaven.*
> *Give us this day our daily bread.*
> *And forgive us our debts,*
> *as we also have forgiven our debtors.*
> *And do not bring us to the time of trial,*
> *but rescue us from the evil one.'*
> (Matthew 6:9-13)

Finally, in his first letter to the Thessalonians this is what Saint Paul had to say about prayer,

'Rejoice always, pray without ceasing, give thanks in all circumstances; for this is the will of God in Christ Jesus for you.' (1 Thessalonians 5:16-18)

Paul's refrain here appears to be, pray constantly and what I am suggesting is that this can be our starting point in our desire to find God, that is, to look for him within ourselves. What we can conclude at this point, I would suggest, is that prayer was very important for Jesus and his relationship with his Father. Equally, Jesus urged all those who came to him to realise that the kingdom of God was, in fact, within them. So where do we start?

Some people will find the prospect of prayer quite daunting in so far as they may never have prayed before in their life. Some people are weighed down by having to high an expectation of themselves when it comes to payer. They seek some kind of mystical experience or instant response or a feel good factor. For me, however, the first rule of prayer is to have no expectations but just to allow God to be God and see what happens. Remember that you might not be used to prayer or you might even be afraid but above all else do not worry. Just keep in mind the fact that you are in good company because we know that Jesus prayed.

The starting point needs to be that you must be yourself and that will always be good enough. Do not fall into the trap of comparing yourself to anyone; this will be between you and God, who knows even the number of hairs on your head. (Matthew 10:30) So, here is what I would suggest you do,

1. Find a quiet place where you can be restful and at peace but alone.

2. Spend some time just listening to yourself trying to discover what is going on within you. What are your concerns and worries? What is making you anxious or afraid? What is preventing you being the person who you really are?

3. Now try to go deep within yourself, keeping those words of Jesus in your mind, *'The Kingdom of Heaven is within you.'*

Look for the deepest, most inward part of your being, search for who you really are.

4. Call to mind now the people who you care about and love and simply, at least for a while, let them go. Reflect truthfully on,

- How alone you are in life?
- How far away you are from people, even those you love?
- What are you really feeling now?

5. Do not be afraid of your feelings, just accept them and keep going deeper and deeper into yourself.

6. Try to remain quiet and still. You are making the journey within, perhaps going to places within yourself that you have never been to before.

7. Now dive deep into the person who you really are, find your true being, your true self. For some people this can be challenging, fearful and even frightening but you have come too far to stop now just keep going. Remember, you are trying to discover,

- Who you really are, not who you think you are.
- Not whom you think you ought to be.
- Not even who you want to be.
- No but who you are, who you really are and always have been, but that person has become buried so deep within you that they are barely recognisable, even to you.
- So, where does this real you come from?

- Where does your life and its source come from?

Now this mystery of your being, of who you really are and always have been, this source of your life is what we call God. Now there is a surprise! If we get this far the next step is crucial and we have to do something really important, let go! Just abandon yourself to this mystery, embrace it but also trust it. However, such trust requires you to be open to its true source, which is God. If you can get this far and if you can do this, no matter how many attempts it takes, something happens, realisation breaks in and you begin to see the truth about yourself, a truth which has always existed but which you have kept at a safe distance within yourself. At this moment when you are confronted with your real self and your eyes are finally opened, you, in fact, wake up, perhaps for the very first time in your life and begin to see things differently. This is the action of grace, God's grace, God's Holy Spirit, working and moving within you. All of a sudden you begin to realise that this God who you thought was unknown or far away is, in fact, nearer to you than you could ever have imagined. That is because *'The Kingdom of Heaven is within you,'* there inside of you dwells the living God. He is the one that holds your fragile self in being. He is the one who is the source of your life. At this point a second realisation becomes possible, which is, unlike the love of people, this God who is the very source of who you are and who gives you life loves you from the inside.

What you are now experiencing again, perhaps for the first time in your life, is the God of the heart, which is the only way to experience the *'Crucified God.'* In this way the very heart of God is speaking to your heart, your true self. Now something else begins to happen because you suddenly begin to realise that your eyes have begun to open, possibly for the first time in your life. As a result you can now begin to see with the eyes of faith and on that day both for you and your life everything changes and nothing can and will ever be the same again. Let us now *see* how this works in action.

Seeing God with the eyes of faith

Every year as we enter the season of Advent I like to pay a visit to the German Christmas market in the centre of Birmingham. If truth be told, I just want to experience the lights, the smells, the food, the music, the people and the atmosphere and in this I am not alone because literally thousands of people come every year. Yet sometimes I just stand there, in the midst of all the activity, and ask myself the question, *'Where is God?'* Is this really Christmas? Is this what Christmas means? Or in the words of John Lennon, *'And so this is Christmas?'* Is this what people really want? Is this what people are really looking for? All of these questions I ask myself but then I go deeper. Has Christmas with its true message about the birth of the Saviour been hijacked, disfigured, repackaged and commercialised as a commodity for people to buy and sell? Where then is the mystery of God which lies at the very heart of the Christmas message? If we are ever going to answer this question in an authentic way, one that speaks directly to us, then we must do so for ourselves. This, however, brings us back to the God that dwells within each and every single one of us. That, as we have seen, is where we have to discover God first, if we are ever going to recognise him anywhere else.

If we are truly to find and experience God in the mystery of Christmas then we have to begin by preparing ourselves. Matthew's Gospel is of great help here because in it we are told, referring to the birth of Jesus, *'and they will call him Immanuel, and name which means God-is-with-us.'* (Matthew 1:23) This, in turn, brings us right back to our original question, *'Where is God?'* and how do we know *'God-is-with-us?'* Once again, to answer this we have to start by looking within ourselves to find the God who dwells in our own heart. This is the God who has always been there, who will never abandon us and who is who we really are. If we can fully realise this then something happens – a revelation – of a truth. That we are and never can be ever truly alone. That is because, in truth, no one is alone because Matthew tells us clearly and unambiguously that, *'God-is-with-us.'* It is here, therefore, that we find the essential message of Christmas, that *'God-is-with-us,'* here and now and forever. Suddenly this is something to celebrate with great joy.

Let us go back now to the Birmingham Christmas German market or any such place and take a good look around. What do you see? Look into the faces of the people and realise an eternal truth, you are, in fact, looking directly at God! Once this happens we suddenly realise what our role and our mission in life really is. You see this belief in God, which we call faith is about our relationship with God in Christ, who is the *'Crucified God.'* The church and its entire people are invited to sacramentally realise this in the way in which we live our lives today. In other words the way in which we live actually matters because it makes present in the here and now the God who dwells within each and every single one of us. In this way God in Christ is sacramentally present in all those men and women who have borne witness to him, filled by the grace of the Holy Spirit, ever since the resurrection.

However, as we realise this truth – stop! Now take a good hard look again, at the Birmingham Christmas German market scene, and notice something that you never really saw before. Look into the shop doorways, dark alleyways and back streets. What do you see? The homeless, the poor, the destitute, all those living with pain, suffering and sadness, whoever and wherever they are. You might have seen them before but now look at them again, only this time see in them the face of God.

If God in Christ is born and lives again in us then we must be like him by reflecting in our lives something of his mercy, compassion, forgiveness and love. Expressing our joy at God's presence in us invites us to be generous to all those who suffer and who also reflect the presence of the *'Crucified God'* in the world today. So when the question is asked, *'Where is God?'* the answer becomes a challenge both to ourselves and the way in which we live our lives. Find him in yourself but love and serve him in others. I bet you never expected that! Matthew begins his Gospel with the words, *'and they will call him Immanuel, and name which means God-is-with-us.'* (Matthew 1:23) but he ends it like this, *'And behold, I am with you always, to the end of time.'* (Matthew 28:20) It is as if he is saying one last time, do not forget where I am, and do not forget where to look for me, for *'I am always with you.'*

CHAPTER THREE

'What is God like?

'No one can have greater love than to lay down his life for his friends.'

(John 15:13)

This must be the one most popular question that I have been ever asked. Whether by children or by adults, whether by people who would profess a religious faith or not, this question has come up time and time again. I remember once reading about a survey, which focused attention on asking this very question, *'What is God like?'* The survey was carried out with young children from a variety of backgrounds without asking if they had a religious belief or not. Once the results came in God was described as an old man with a beard, dressed in white and living in the clouds. The same survey was then repeated, with the same children many years later when they had reached adulthood. The conclusions, however, remained exactly the same, in so far as God was still described as an old man with a beard, dressed in white and living in the clouds. In other words nothing had changed, their perception of God had remained exactly the same. What did emerge from the survey, however, was a harmless, comforting and somewhat irrelevant image of God, that appeared to satisfy both young and old alike but which had very little impact on their lives. Some people on the other hand see God as a judge or a vengeful father who stores up all our records of wrong with the intention of making us pay when the day of judgement arrives. Others see God as distant as not really being interested in our day-to-day lives but only in the mistakes that we make. Some even see God as a prop or an idea, which helps us cope with the daily difficulties and problems of life. Of course there are also those people who reject the very idea of God as being nothing less than fictitious nonsense. Perhaps now you might reflect upon your own belief in God or whether you, in fact, believe in God or not. So if you were asked the question, *'What is God like?'* How would you answer it? What would you say? Give yourself some time to reflect on the question and just answer it in as honest a way as possible. Just remember you do not have to please anyone, this is not a test but it is, for you the reader, a starting point.

The title of this book is *'Only in the Crucified God,'* and an understanding of what this means is a theme which, understandably, runs all the way through it. However, there are, in fact, many ways to try and understand what this means and what this tells us about what God is like. So I am going to start my answer to this question with some words from Saint Paul from his letter to the Philippians where, perhaps, he himself is quoting from an ancient Christian hymn which sheds light on what God is, in fact, like.

'Who, though he was in the form of God,
did not regard equality with God
as something to be exploited,
but emptied himself,
taking the form of a slave,
being born in human likeness.
And being found in human form,
he humbled himself
and became obedient to the point of death —
even death on a cross.
Therefore God also highly exalted him
and gave him the name
that is above every name,
so that at the name of Jesus
every knee should bend,
in heaven and on earth and under the earth,
and every tongue should confess
that Jesus Christ is Lord,
to the glory of God the Father.' (Philippians 2:6-11)

Read this passage through slowly to yourself and see if it says anything directly to you. Do you have an image of God, which emerges out of these words, a picture which comes into your mind or touches your heart, which says, this is what God is like? How does it make you feel? Perhaps nothing happens at all. Just remember that we are exploring this question together and different people will have different starting points. So if nothing happens, do not worry about it. We are only at the beginning of our journey.

The passage is about Jesus, who for Christians is the Son of God. Right from the beginning we are left in no doubt that this Jesus is, in fact, God. Then something remarkable happens because we are told that this God literally empties himself. That is to say he leaves his divinity behind to become not only one like us, but actually one of us, one with us, to be born just like us, to live just like us and ultimately to die, just like us. Yet not just any death but one, which would involve total humiliation, total abandonment and pain and suffering beyond anything we could ever begin to imagine. In the end death would be his fate just as it is ours but that is not the end of the story, indeed far from it. For he will be raised up from the grave and recognised for whom he really is Jesus Christ, the Lord. Now we are just beginning to understand what this Crucified God is like and what he is prepared to do for us. Though the burning question still remains as to why God would do such a thing?

I now want us to explore our question about, *'What is God like?'* a little further but in a different though no less profound way. To do this I want us to explore a story together which as you read it I would ask that you look for links between Paul's quotation above and what the story might be telling us about what God is actually like.

The Shepherd and the King

There was once a great King who, as you can imagine, had everything in life anyone could possibly ever want. One day he called to him his wisest advisors and asked them a question,
'I want you to tell me what God is like?'

They seemed unsure and found it difficult to give him an answer. So the King said,

'Right I'm going to give you one week, after which I want you to assemble the Grand Council in the Great Hall. I want the cleverest people in my kingdom to be summoned and I want them to tell me what God is like!'

One week went by and the Grand Council assembled in the Great Hall. The King stood up and addressed them all,

'I will give each group here the chance to address this council only once. All you have to do is tell me what God is like. Do I make myself clear?'

'Yes my Lord,' they all replied.

The scientists were chosen to go first and their speaker stood up and addressed all those assembled,

'It is impossible to prove that God exists but equally it is impossible to prove that God does not exist. There are many scientific theories about the world and how it works just as there are many great scientists who have devoted their lives to advancing our knowledge and understanding of the universe. We now know more about our world than we have ever known before and our knowledge continues to expand.'

At this point the King interrupted,

'Yes that's all very well but can you tell me what God is actually like? Yes or no?'

'No my Lord, that's not possible for us to do,' answered the scientist.

'Then I suggest you sit down,' replied the King.

The next to speak up were the philosophers, lawyers and politicians. Their speaker stood up and addressed the assembly as follows,

'We are people of the mind. We debate, we discuss, we think, we argue and we theorise. We try to make sense out of our world. We try to reconcile people and avoid conflict. We make every effort to make the world in which

we live a better place for all people, a fairer place a more just place. We are people who dedicate our lives to higher principles, who recognise both human dignity and uniqueness. We are ……..'

At this point the King interrupted,

'All very good and noble,' he said, 'but can you tell us all what God is like?'

There was no reply at this point.

'Then I suggest you sit down,' said the King.

Finally it was the turn of the theologians, so called experts on God to speak.

'My Lord King we know that God is omnipotent, omniscient and omnipresent. That he is all powerful, all knowing and all present.'

'Yes but I challenge you now before all these assembled guests to tell me what God is like?' interrupted the King. 'Now in simple and straightforward language can you do it or not?' he went on.

'We cannot,' replied the speaker for the theologians.

At this point the King stood up and addressed all those present.

'Enough of this waffle, I do not know why you all could not have said in the first place that we cannot tell you what God is like because we do not know. Instead your pride and arrogance prevented you all from doing so. Shame on you! So here is my proclamation. Send out a message to the whole of my kingdom, that one year from today this Council will reassemble and that I will give a huge reward to anyone who can tell me what God is like. Do I make myself clear?'

'Yes my Lord,' they all replied.

Now one year went by and once again the Grand Council assembled in the Great Hall. The King stood up and addressed all those who were present, 'Has anyone come to tell me what God is like?' he asked.

Only silence was his reply. Then one of his servants approached him and whispered in his ear,

'My lord King there is a Shepherd outside who claims he can tell you what God is like but he is afraid that if he does so you will punish him.'

'Nonsense,' replied the King. 'Show him in and tell him there will be no such punishment, I give him my word.'

Moments later the doors to the great hall opened and in walked a Shepherd. He was bare-footed and filthy dirty, dressed in little more than rags, with a shepherd's crook held firmly in one hand. As he approached the throne the assembled crowd began to laugh,

'Silence,' shouted the King. 'I will have silence in this hall!'

Standing before the King, sitting on his throne, the Shepherd looked up directly into his face, his own eyes a deep shade of blue, his face wrinkled and burnt by the sun.

'Now,' began the King, 'I'm told you can tell me and all these good people assembled here what God is like. Can you do that for us?'

'I can your majesty,' the Shepherd replied.

However, once again laughter rang out amongst the assembled gathering. The King now stood up and spoke directly to them all,

'I will say this one more time. This man will be heard and if you show him disrespect one more time I will not only have you removed from this hall but removed from office as well. Do I make myself abundantly clear?'

'Yes my Lord,' they all replied.

'Now proceed,' the King said to the Shepherd.

'My Lord King I am afraid that if in front of all these guests I show you what God is like you will punish me,' said the Shepherd.

'Punish you said the King. No my friend I will not punish you, I will reward you, and I swear it before all these people. Now please proceed.'

'In which case,' continued the Shepherd, 'we both need to do something.'
'Name it,' said the King. 'Name it and it will be done,' he continued.
'My Lord King you and I need to exchange clothes and swap places,' said
the Shepherd.
In response to these words the whole of the assembly gasped in disbelief.
The King, however, stood up, and came down from his throne and started
to remove his clothes, whilst the Shepherd did the same with his. Slowly
the King put on the filthy rags of the Shepherd whilst the Shepherd adorned
himself in the royal robes. Finally the King took off his crown and placed
onto the head of the Shepherd who sat down gingerly on the throne. The
whole crowd now looked on in total silence. Finally the Shepherd from his
position on the throne dressed in the full regalia of the King said,
'My Lord, this is what God is like.'
Then to the shock and amazement of all those present, the King knelt
before his own throne and the Shepherd who sat upon it, finally realising
that this was, in fact, exactly what God is really like.

What this simple story does is focus on an understanding of God that we do not expect. This is the God who behaves in a completely different way, which does not conform to the attributes we might be tempted to attach to him. There is no power here, no glory, no control or manipulation. Instead what we do find is humility and meekness. The story seems to reverse that of Paul's letter to the Philippians and yet, at the same time, reveals exactly the same thing about God. Here the shepherd reveals his true identity as King who gave his kingship up to reveal the true nature of God. Whilst the King learns what God is really like only by giving his kingship up. God is not what we expect him to be. God does not act in the way we expect him to act. Keeping this firmly in mind we can now go back to the scriptures and focus our attention, once again, on Jesus.

In the Gospel of John we find a remarkable statement, *'No one has ever seen God.'* (John 1:18) Yet the same text goes on to say, *'it is the only Son (Jesus), who is close to the Father's heart, who has made him known.'* (John 1:18) Going back then to our reflection on Saint Paul's letter to the Philippians it is through Jesus that the Christian comes to know what God is really like. Let us make no mistake here, Jesus is not just another prophet nor does he speak only for God. No, he is in fact the Word of God made man, *'In the beginning was the Word: the Word was with God and the Word was God.'* (John 1:1) In fact, *'The Word became flesh, he lived among us, and we saw his glory, the glory that he has from the Father as the only Son of the Father, full of grace and truth.'* (John 1:14) This means that we can now say that in his person Jesus actually reveals what God is like. His life is nothing less than the living parable of God himself. Thus through his life, teaching and ministry Jesus unveils the nature and the very being of God right before our very eyes.

As a result if we really want to know what God is like then we must look first and foremost to Jesus because he makes present and visible the invisible mystery of God, as he in and of himself possesses the fullness of divinity. Yet just as Paul described it and as we can clearly see in the story of the *'Shepherd and the King'* Jesus actually lets go of his divine status and becomes the man for others. Now in his life and ministry not only does he announce and proclaim the imminence of the Kingdom of God but lives it out in his own life. Through him we see the depth of God's love for us when he freely gives up his own life. Therefore if we have the courage and are really willing to seek an answer to the question, *'What is God like?'* then by focusing our attention on Jesus our flawed understanding of God will be healed by and through him.

When we turn to Jesus then what do we actually find in terms of him revealing what God is really like? Firstly, his life, his teachings, his parables, and his miracles all bear witness to the presence of the kingdom of God. Now let us, in turn, see what picture of God emerges. What you will find is a merciful Father, the Father of forgiveness, the Father of compassion and above all the Father of love. However, the full depth of this love and the deepest revelation of God comes through the death of his Son Jesus on the cross. Here we see the unconditional and infinite love of God most fully revealed. Once again John tells us, *'For God so loved the world that he gave his only Son.'* (John 3:16) Jesus also said in his ministry, *'No one can have greater love than to lay down his life for his friends.'* (John 15:13) This, in fact, is exactly why this book is called, *'Only in the Crucified God'* because it is in the figure of Jesus on the cross that we come to know, ultimately, what God is really like. Yet the love of God reaches even beyond death and raises the Son to new life. The gift of the Holy Spirit, which comes directly from God, then comes to us so that he dwells within each and every single one of us making us all members of the one family. It is this truth, which compels me to write these words and inspires all those who follow Jesus to recognise and serve him in one another just as he did.

The wholly different and radical nature of this new way of understanding what God is like turns the values of the world on its head. You ask me what God is like and I reply by inviting you to look at Jesus and discover something quite remarkable. For in him God comes to us in the weakness and vulnerability of our own flesh and blood and makes himself completely susceptible to our helplessness to the point where he even suffers and dies. What we are saying then is Jesus reveals God not in power but in weakness and helplessness. Why would God do this you may ask? The only answer is love. God's power is to be found only in love. Yet this love suffered and died to reveal its true nature. It could be said, therefore, that there is only one type of suffering, God's and that all our suffering whatever form it may take is nothing less than a participation in God's suffering. This means that God is never absent from our pain and suffering but is to be found in the midst of it. Yet beyond suffering there is life. We call it the resurrection and it is God's supreme gift of love to all people. If we really want to know what God is like, think of it like this. Out of love God chose the path of pain and suffering so that we could share in his life, therefore intimately knowing him and participating in his very nature and being for all time; for he is the God of mercy, the God compassion, the God forgiveness and above all the God of love – that, therefore is what God is like.

CHAPTER FOUR

'Does God Love Everyone?' Part One

'My son you are with me always and all I have is yours. But it was only right we should celebrate and rejoice, because your brother here was dead and has come to life; he was lost and is found.' (Luke 15: 31-32)

This is another one of those questions that Jesus actually answers for himself through a parable, a story with a meaning. Now when Jesus told these parables he rarely explained what they meant, this is because he wanted people to work that out for themselves, which is not easy to do. However, when we turn to the Holy Spirit and are guided by God's grace something wonderful happens because we are drawn deeper and deeper not only into the mystery of God but also into the mystery of what that means for us. This approach though is challenging because what we discover might surprise us and invite us to change our whole perspective on the nature and being of God. This is because Jesus actually confronts humanity with a different way of being. Only by actually experiencing God's love alone can we ever begin to understand what that means for us and the way in which we are invited to live our lives. What we discover is shocking and revelatory shaking our accepted values to their core but what emerges is something better, something purer, nothing less than an invitation to participate in the very life of God himself.

We can now begin to explore such a parable. To begin with just read the words through slowly to yourself and, as you come to the end, ask yourself the question, '*What does this mean?*'

The Labourers in the Vineyard (Matthew 20: 1-16)

"For the kingdom of heaven is like a landowner who went out early in the morning to hire labourers for his vineyard. After agreeing with the labourers for the usual daily wage, he sent them into his vineyard. When he went out about nine o'clock, he saw others standing idle in the marketplace; and he said to them, 'You also go into the vineyard, and I will pay you whatever is right.' So they went. When he went out again about noon and about three o'clock, he did the same. And about five o'clock he went out and found others standing around; and he said to them, 'Why are you standing here idle all day?' They said to him, 'Because no one has hired us.' He said to them, 'You also go into the vineyard.' When evening came, the owner of the vineyard said to his manager, 'Call the labourers and give them their pay, beginning with the last and then going to the first.' When those hired about five o'clock came, each of them received the usual daily wage. Now when the first

came, they thought they would receive more; but each of them also received the usual daily wage. And when they received it, they grumbled against the landowner, saying, 'These last worked only one hour, and you have made them equal to us who have borne the burden of the day and the scorching heat.' But he replied to one of them, 'Friend, I am doing you no wrong; did you not agree with me for the usual daily wage? Take what belongs to you and go; I choose to give to this last the same as I give to you. Am I not allowed to do what I choose with what belongs to me? Or are you envious because I am generous?' So the last will be first, and the first will be last."

The first thing to note about this parable is how outrageous it is in the way in which it seems to undermine our sense of fairness. The workers who had been in the fields all day are paid exactly the same amount as those who came late. Here we find ourselves sympathising with the former who upon receiving their wages grumbled, *'These last worked only one hour, and you have made them equal to us who have borne the burden of the day and the scorching heat.'* But now note the reply of the landowner, *'Friend, I am doing you no wrong; did you not agree with me for the usual daily wage? Take what belongs to you and go; I choose to give to this last the same as I give to you. Am I not allowed to do what I choose with what belongs to me? Or are you envious because I am generous?'*

So what exactly is going on here? How can we make any kind of sense, at all, out of this parable? Well, if you take the time to return to your Bible you will notice that what follows directly after this parable in Matthew's Gospel is Jesus's prediction of his passion when he says, *'See, we are going up to Jerusalem, and the Son of Man will be handed over to the chief priests and scribes, and they will condemn him to death; then they will hand him over to the Gentiles to be mocked and flogged and crucified; and on the third day he will be raised.'* Is there a link, therefore, between the parable and Jesus's predication of his own death and if so what is it? To make this connection we need to hold together two things:

1. In the parable the land owner is God, the labourers are people and the wages represent God's overwhelming generosity and love given freely and equally to all the workers and therefore to all people, without exception.
2. When Jesus predicts his passion and death he is describing the complete humiliation of God's Messiah, His chosen or anointed one.

Both of these statements push at the very boundaries of our understanding of God and what that actually means. So does God, in effect, love all people? Yes! What about those who do not practice their faith? Yes! What about those who do not believe in him? Yes! What about those who have never heard of him? Yes! What about those people who reject him? Yes! God loves all people equally; this is the very essence of this parable. This was a lesson Peter had to learn for himself when he said, *'I truly understand that God has no favourites,'* (Acts 10:34). However, note what kind of reaction this attitude very often calls forth in us – resentment, jealousy and a complete lack of generosity. And yet here we have it in a parable told by Jesus himself that **God loves all people equally!** It is not ambiguous, it is not uncertain but it is very clear that this is the nature and the being of God and this is what God invites us to share in.

But the story does not end there. God will draw us deeper into understanding what this really means. This is because the link between the parable and the cross is essential in our understanding of who and what God is. The generosity of God, the very love of God will result in the crucifixion of His Son. But this death would, contrary to the religious beliefs of the day, reveal God's love for all people, the whole of humanity. Just as in the parable Jesus reveals that God loves all people equally leaving no one out; so in his death he embraces the whole of humanity itself even those who feel themselves rejected, despised and unwanted by God. Think for a moment of the words of Peter in Luke, *'Leave me Lord; I am a sinful man.'* (Luke 5:8) or of the prophet Isaiah, *'What a wretched state I am in! I am lost, for I am a man of unclean lips,'* (Isaiah 6:5) both of whom saw themselves as ungodly at the time when in truth they were both loved by God beyond anything they could ever imagine. As always this brings us ultimately back to the *'Crucified God'* and what this means for humanity.

What we are dealing with here then is something almost beyond our comprehension to both understand and accept that God does, in fact, love all people unconditionally. Yet from the beginning this is the way it has always been. God's covenant with Abraham was unconditional with God starting the covenant and completing it by playing the role of both parties – the weaker one as well as the stronger. (Genesis 15: 17-21)

In conclusion then what Jesus does is that he both confronts us with and at the same time reveals the nature and the being of God's unconditional love for all people. Such love is very often beyond our ability to grasp let alone do and yet it is here in the words of scripture, right before our very eyes. So when I am asked the question, *'Does God love all people?'* My answer is always a resounding, *'Yes.'* And when the follow up questions comes, *'How do you know?'* I reply by saying, *'Because God both tells us and shows us.'* Now what that means for us, and the way in which we live our lives will become the subject of our next reflection.

'Does God Love Everyone?' Part Two

Our task now will be to explore what this means for the way in which we live our lives. It is vitally important to understand how God's universal, all-inclusive, unconditional love impacts on life here and now. However, we do this from the premise that God does, in fact, love all people without exception even those who reject him. To do this we will explore another parable told by Jesus called *'Lost Son'* (Luke 15: 11-32). There is no other parable in the whole of the New Testament like this one for the way in which it profoundly delves deep into the mystery of both God and what it means to be human. At the same time there is also no other parable as relevant as this, for us today, for revealing the full depth of the Father who simply loves.

Once again I invite you, the reader, to slowly and carefully read through the parable asking yourself, *'What does this mean and how is it relevant to my life today?'*

The Lost Son (Luke 15:11-32)

Then Jesus said, "There was a man who had two sons. The younger of them said to his father, 'Father, give me the share of the property that will belong to me.' So he divided his property between them. A few days later the younger son gathered all he had and travelled to a distant country, and there he squandered his property in dissolute living. When he had spent everything, a severe famine took place throughout that country, and he began to be in need. So he went and hired himself out to one of the citizens of that country, who sent him to his fields to feed the pigs. He would gladly have filled himself with the pods that the pigs were eating; and no one gave him anything. But when he came to himself he said, 'How many of my father's hired hands have bread enough and to spare, but here I am dying of hunger! I will get up and go to my father, and I will say to him, "Father, I have sinned against heaven and before you, I am no longer worthy to be called your son; treat me like one of your hired hands."' So he set off and went to his father. But while he was still far off, his father saw him and was filled with compassion; he ran and put his arms around him and kissed him. Then the son said to him, 'Father, I have sinned against heaven and before you; I am no longer worthy to be called your so.' But the father said to his slaves, 'Quickly, bring out a robe—the best one—and put it on him; put a ring on his finger and sandals on his feet And get the fatted calf and kill it, and let us eat and celebrate; for this son of mine was dead and is alive again; he was lost and is found!' And they began to celebrate.

"Now his elder son was in the field; and when he came and approached the house, he heard music and dancing. He called one of the slaves and asked what was going on. He replied, 'Your brother has come, and your father has killed the fatted calf, because he has got him back safe and sound.' Then he became angry and refused to go in. His father came out and began to plead with him. But he answered his father, 'Listen! For all these years I have been working like a slave for you, and I have never disobeyed your command; yet you have never given me even a young goat so that I might celebrate with my friends. But when this son of yours came back, who has devoured your property with prostitutes, you killed the fatted calf for him!' Then the father said to him, 'Son, you

are always with me, and all that is mine is yours. But we had to celebrate and rejoice, because this brother of yours was dead and has come to life; he was lost and has been found.'"

The first thing to note about this parable is how unusual the Farther is. In the ancient world it was common practice, on death, for the whole of the estate to pass, from the father, to the eldest son, with nothing going to any other brother. This Father, however, is different because he has made it clear that when he dies the estate is to be divided equally between his two sons. However, his younger son comes to him and asks for his share of the estate now! In doing so he is, therefore, expressing a desire for his Father to be dead. In other words he wants to be free, to break all ties with his Father, yet this can only happen if his Father passes away. Without a single word of protest his Father grants him his wish. In this way he is allowing his son to be free, to choose his own future. Here right at the beginning of the parable we get a sense of just how different this Father is as we see right before our very eyes his overwhelming generosity as an expression of the love he has for his son.

If we take this a little deeper there is something else going on here that Jesus wants to draw our attention to. In the parable the Father represents God and his two sons' people. Concentrating our attention on the relationship between the younger son and his Father what we are witnessing here is nothing less than a rejection of God. The younger son is expressing a desire to free from God to, in effect, have nothing to do with him. Is this so different from the world in which we live today? At least in the western world many people have made a conscious or unconscious decision to be free from God, to live life as if he did not exist.

Indeed there is increasing pressure to remove God from society and from our moral consciences. In the parable the Father remains silent. In the world when people choose to abandon or reject God, once again the Father remains silent. People must choose God for themselves, there cannot be, there will not be any sense, at all, of being forced.

Returning to the parable we are told that the next action of the son is to get as far away from his Father as possible when he goes to a distant country. Here he can be free to do whatever he wants, to live however he wants and to choose whatever he wants. Now the Father sees his son go and although he does not travel with him in a physical sense, his heart never leaves him. Indeed, every morning he will go out and wait patiently for him to return but this is something his son must freely choose to do himself. In the same way the modern world appears to be withdrawing further and further away from God so that for some he is becoming little more than a distant memory. Yet in and through this parable Jesus is teaching us that the Father is always with us, always loving us even those who choose to reject him.

In this distant land the son now adopts a new life, without his Father, which involves wild living. His new life is based on self. He now lives for self-pleasure and self-satisfaction. There is no room for the morality of the Father in this new world order. Instead life will be lived totally on his terms. As a result it will be chaotic and disordered. Time now has no meaning until one day it all comes crashing down and his new world comes to a sharp end. With famine devastating the land he is forced to work with pigs, an animal described as unclean and forbidden to all Jews in the Hebrew Scriptures. Eventually when he reaches his lowest point he cries out, *'Here I am dying of hunger.'*

Perhaps there comes that moment in life for all us, no matter what we have, when we realise that there is something fundamental missing in our lives. Something deep within ourselves that needs to be fulfilled, a hunger, a yearning or a void the first sign of which is to recognise our need for love. Such a moment can also be the first sign of our distance from God. We know we lack something. We know that there is a void within our hearts. We know that we appear to have all that we want, even our freedom but still something remains unfulfilled deep within us without which, we know, that we are not truly alive. What then is it that we still hunger and desire for?

In the parable we are told that the young man eventually came to his senses. He managed to recognise that deep emptiness within himself and what did he see there, what did he recognise? The face of his Father! Suddenly he was reminded of all those things he had associated with his Father but had, up until now, completely forgotten, the food, the house and all that love. Then finally he concluded, here I am starving to death. Now something happens within him and a new desire emerges, only this time it is freedom not without his Father but with him. He recognises his mistakes, accepts them and makes a decision, in freedom, for himself, that he will go back to his Father.

As the son returns home and tries to say sorry for his mistakes he is overwhelmed by the Father's love. The cloak, the ring, the sandals, the food are all symbols meant to represent the abundance of the Father's love for his son. For in truth although his son abandoned and rejected him the Father never, ever stopped loving him. As the two embrace, probably in floods of tears, I cannot help but reflect on how the son must have concluded that the freedom he had coveted at the beginning, in reality, he had always had.

In this parable Jesus reveals what God the Father is really like. This is a God who loves everyone, even those who reject him. This is a God who on the return of his son, ran to meet him, threw his arms around him and kisses him. This is the God that Jesus came to reveal. This is the God that Jesus wants us to know. As we come to the end of this part of the reflection I cannot help but wonder that if people really knew God in this way how many of those who have chosen to reject him would in the same way freely choose to return to a Father who has never stopped loving them.

Does God Love Everyone? Part Three

A personal reflection

Having clearly established, through scripture, how, in fact, God does literally love everyone I now want to explore what this means in practice. I am going to do this through reflecting on a personal experience of my own, drawing on the parables we have just explored together.

There is a family I know very well who, if truth be told, would not describe themselves as religious or believers in God. At the heart of this family was a man who held everything together. He was a husband, a father and a grandfather who had, himself, suffered his own tragedies in life. One of his daughters' died when she was in her mid-thirties and later her daughter and therefore his granddaughter also died in her early twenties whilst pregnant. Thankfully, however, the child survived. There was also another granddaughter who had also died without ever having left hospital after she was born. All this meant that he found life, personally, hard to cope with and God, for him, therefore was not even on his radar. Perhaps, we can understand and sympathise why this was the case as life can be both hard and cruel at times. Then one day he became seriously ill and was taken into hospital. The family asked me, as a minister of the church, if I would go? What was I to say, '*No*?' Surely here, in this moment, we find the God who loves all people, even those who do not consciously believe in him. Perhaps by asking me, as a minister of the church, I thought, this was their way of expressing a faith known only to God himself.

When I arrived at the hospital I found one of those heart-breaking scenes that is only too familiar to ministers of the church. The family were crowded round the bed, many of them in tears, begging the man not to go, not to leave them. He was obviously seriously ill by now and deteriorating, with an oxygen mask attached to his face as he struggled to breath. I did the only thing I could do, pray and offer him a blessing. Yet there was something else going on here, at a deeper level that, somehow, through my faith and my presence the love of God was also made present too. Just as in the parable of the lost son, the Father's heart went out to the family gathered around that bed in a distant country far away from the church and institutionalised religion. For God still loved this family and God was still with them and it was my role to make that a visible and a tangible reality. To watch others suffer like this is to see the *'Crucified God'* before our very eyes because in the pain, the isolation and in the feelings of desolation experienced by those present; God lives.

A few days later I was called back to the hospital because sadly the man had died. Once again the family were broken hearted and in truth I was too, for the minister is called to suffer with God's people just as Christ did himself. Members of the family were now literally terrified to see the man now that he was dead. I understood that because it is not an easy thing to do at such a vulnerable time. Peoples' image of their loved one is of happiness and health and they do not want such memories to be tarnished. However, there was a need coming from them for someone to be with him, for someone to do something. Again was this an expression of a faith, known only to God? Needless to say I went in and spent some time with the gentleman. I placed a crucifix gently on his forehead, prayed for him and the family before finally giving him a blessing. The family found consolation in this and once again I became profoundly aware of the God who does not abandon his people because he loves them more deeply and more intimately than any of us could ever know.

Finally, I was asked to take the funeral. It was for me, as it always is when people ask me to do something like this an absolute privilege. Funerals by their very nature are never easy but when it is someone that you know and familiar faces and friends all with broken hearts surround you, it becomes really emotionally demanding. The one thing that does not change, however, is God. The *'Crucified God'* is the God who suffers with his people, who is broken hearted with his people and who enters the darkness of death and the grave with his people. This God never abandons the subjects of his love. This God loves continually and unconditionally and in the brokenness of life, in the darkness of death and in the sorrow of grief he and he alone brings life. So I reflected on the man's life and reminded the family of the many good times they shared together. I preached about death not being the end but only the beginning of a new life in Christ. Finally, I offered consolation in reflecting on a ship as it slowly moved towards the horizon, getting smaller and smaller until in the end it disappeared. Although we cannot see that ship anymore we know that it is still there. In the same way, when somebody dies they may no longer be physically with us, because they are dead to this life but our faith tells us that they are alive in Christ who himself said, *'I am the resurrection. If anyone believes in me, even though he dies he will live, and whoever lives and believes in me will never die.' (John 11: 26)* As I came to the end of the homily I finally left an image with the family of the man who, though we could not see him, was just over the horizon with his daughter and granddaughters waiting for the day when we will all be reunited again. God is love, God's nature is to love and God only knows love. This was and is the essential message of Jesus as revealed through the *'Crucified God.'* It was a message so dear to Jesus's heart that he constantly made the same point over and over again through his parables until in the end he had to make that love physically present for all to see in his crucifixion. It is this love that sustains our faith and our lives today. For in answer to the question, *'Does God love everyone?'* The answer quite simply is, *'Yes.'*

CHAPTER FIVE

'What is faith?'

'Do not let your hearts be troubled. Trust in God, trust also in me'

(John 14:1)

In the Gospel of Luke the disciples ask Jesus, *'Increase our faith.'* (Luke 17:5) In Mark Jesus says, *'Everything is possible for the one who has faith.'* (Mark 9:24) The difficulty, however, is that we are tempted to say that we know what faith is, believing in God without the requirement of proof. But is that good enough to satisfy our enquiring minds? In the passage we have just referred to from Mark a father asks Jesus to help his son who is possessed by a demon. The father responds to Jesus's words about faith by replying, *'I have faith. Help my lack of faith.'* (Mark 9:25) This brings us back to our question then, *'What is faith?'* How we proceed from this point on will be crucial in trying to explain exactly what we mean by faith.

As Christians our starting point always has to be with Jesus and if we explore his life, work and ministry in the Gospels we soon begin to see how crucial faith in him is.

'Immediately he made the disciples get into the boat and go on ahead to the other side, while he dismissed the crowds. And after he had dismissed the crowds, he went up the mountain by himself to pray. When evening came, he was there alone, but by this time the boat, battered by the waves, was far from the land, for the wind was against them. And early in the morning he came walking toward them on the sea. But when the disciples saw him walking on the sea, they were terrified, saying, "It is a ghost!" And they cried out in fear. But immediately Jesus spoke to them and said, "Take heart, it is I; do not be afraid."

Peter answered him, "Lord, if it is you, command me to come to you on the water." He said, "Come." So Peter got out of the boat, started walking on the water, and came toward Jesus. But when he noticed the strong wind, he became frightened, and beginning to sink, he cried out, "Lord, save me!" Jesus immediately reached out his hand and caught him, saying to him, "You of little faith, why did you doubt?" When they got into the boat, the wind ceased. And those in the boat worshiped him, saying, "Truly you are the Son of God." (Matthew 14:22-33)

In this passage Peter in fact, represents the perfect image of the believer as he walks on the water of the lake towards Jesus. As long he places all his hope and trust in him and in his word all is well but the minute he becomes afraid and loses that trust he sinks beneath the waves. Once his confidence, faith and trust is undermined all becomes lost until, once again, he calls out, *'Lord save me!'*

In another passage Jesus and his disciples are on a boat and a violent storm suddenly erupts threatening to engulf them beneath the waves. The disciples are afraid but Jesus is asleep in the stern of the boat with his head gently resting on a cushion. *'They woke him and said to him, "Master, do you not care? We are lost!"'*(Mark 4:39) At which point Jesus gets up and calms the storm but afterwards says to his disciples, *'Why are you so frightened? Have you still no faith?'* (Mark 4:40) Faith it would seem is crucial to understanding our relationship with Jesus and therefore God. Indeed Jesus actually says quite clearly, *'Do not let your hearts be troubled. Trust in God, trust also in me.'* (John 14:1) Yet we still need to dig deeper if we are to actually understand what this means and what it requires of us.

In the story of the *'Lost Son'* (Luke 15:11-32) the eldest son might define faith in a very different way. For him faith is sticking by the Father, never leaving him, working hard day in and day out, being obedient and following all the rules expected of a loyal and trustworthy son. For him it is as if faith can be earned or that faith is deserved or his by right but is that true? Just look at how he feels about his younger brother, is there any forgiveness, compassion or reconciliation? On the other hand faith for the younger son might be seen as something very different. Faith is being free to choose to love the Father whilst also being free to choose to reject him. In the parable the younger son chooses to come back to a Father he abandoned and rejected a long time ago trusting in his mercy, compassion, forgiveness and love. The main difference between the two sons appears to be in them deciding how to let God be God. Is it on their own terms or his? Because this then leads us to an even greater question, in whom do we really place our faith is it in God or in ourselves? Indeed, if for the purposes of faith we define what that is according to our own criteria are we, in fact, actually preventing God from being God?

At this point look again at the *'Labourers in the vineyard.'* (Matthew 20: 1-16) Those who have been working all day believe that they deserve more than those who were hired at the end of the day. The owner of the vineyard addresses their concerns with these words, *'Take your earnings and go. I choose to pay the latecomer as much as I pay you. Have I no right to do what I like with my own? Why should you be envious because I am generous? Thus the last will be first and the first will be last.'* (Matthew 20:14-16) We need, therefore, to be very careful about whom this God is in which Jesus asks us to place all our trust. Do we allow God to be the God of mercy, compassion, forgiveness and love and all that entails or do we create a God made more in our own image and really place our faith in that instead?

There is a wonderful, if little known, passage in the Old Testament that helps us understand our own tendencies in our relationship with God a little better. It comes from one of the Minor Prophets but is never the less very important,

> *O Lord, how long shall I cry for help,*
> *and you will not listen?*
> *Or cry to you "Violence!"*
> *and you will not save?*
> *Why do you make me see wrongdoing*
> *and look at trouble?*

Destruction and violence are before me;
strife and contention arise.

(Habakkuk 1:2-3)

The first part is really, a rant or complaint from the Prophet. God is not doing what the Prophet wants him to do. God is not conforming to the way in which the prophet wants him to behave. In this respect his prayers, pleas, lamentations, petitions and intercessions are pointless if God simply will not do what the prophet wants him to do. Is the Prophet questioning his faith in a God who appears to do nothing? Why is God silent? Why is there no answer? I wonder how many times in our own lives we have felt exactly like this? How many times we have empathised with the older son in the parable of the *'Lost Son?'* How many times we have just wanted God to do what we want? Is this wrong? Is this faith?

Then the Lord answered me and said:
Write the vision;
make it plain on tablets,
so that a runner may read it.
For there is still a vision for the appointed time;
it speaks of the end, and does not lie.
If it seems to tarry, wait for it;
it will surely come, it will not delay.
Look at the proud!
Their spirit is not right in them,
but the righteous live by their faith.

(Habakkuk 2:2-4)

Now we have God's response and putting it simply what we discover is that no matter what is going on in the world or in our own lives, no matter how dark or how difficult things appear to be we are required to put all our hope and all our trust in Him. This is because God and God alone knows the end of the story, including our own and *'the righteous live by their faith.'*

What is true though is that we have all known periods of intense darkness and sadness in our lives and when such clouds descend we are tempted to ask, *'Where are you God? Why don't you just do something, anything?'* Such times become even more intense when innocence is involved. Once again we can be driven to the very edges of our understanding by demanding, *'Why?'* When this happens we are confronted with the silence of God or what appears to be his absence. So what then of faith and our attempt to define what it is?

There are, in fact, two stories, found in the Old Testament, which throw some light, quite intentionally, on this struggle. The first is to be found in the book of the Prophet Jonah. Putting it simply Jonah, a prophet called by God, to speak on his behalf is angry because although he believes in God nobody else appears to. Instead the world has turned its back on its creator and fallen into a life of immorality and debauchery. As a result Jonah wants God to act, to do something, anything to make things right even if that means punishment. However, God remains silent, which angers the prophet even more, sounds familiar? In the end, God does act by calling the prophet and sending him to Nineveh the most depraved city of all.

Although Jonah is relieved that finally God is actually going to do something he knows all about Nineveh and has no intention of going anywhere near the place, so instead he takes himself off in the opposite direction. This is when eventually he is swallowed up by a large fish and finds himself, when the fish releases him, close to the city of Nineveh. Now Jonah gets it. He will go to the city and preach repentance to the population there but he expects God to punish all those who turn their backs on him and the message he has been invited to proclaim.

Remarkably, however, the people of Nineveh, including the King repent, on hearing his words, in sackcloth and ashes. As a result God shows them mercy and compassion by forgiving them. Jonah is outraged, remember the oldest son in the parable? In fact he is so angry he takes himself out into the desert to die. God, however, makes a plant grow to give him shade and shelter from the sun for which Jonah is grateful. Then God sends a worm, which destroys the plant, and once again Jonah is outraged. The story ends by comparing the compassion, mercy and forgiveness of God to the people of Nineveh with Jonah's anger at the death of his beloved plant! Why is it not possible for the Prophet to rejoice in the repentant sinners of Nineveh? Perhaps for the same reason that the oldest son does not rejoice in the return of his younger brother. In both stories what we see is an inability for humanity to prefer the compassion, mercy and forgiveness of God to its desire for punishment and revenge.

Perhaps when bad things do happen and we are confronted with the apparent silence and absence of God we are tempted to fill the empty space with what we feel should happen. Look at Jonah and the oldest son in the parable for example. There is a wonderful line in the Psalms, which sums this up, inviting us not to *'harden our hearts.'* (Psalm 95:8) The letter to the Hebrews puts it like this, *'If only you would listen to him today; do not harden your hearts.'* (Hebrews 3:15) When we harden our hearts then we expect God to behave in the way we want him to and, as a result, refuse to recognise the God of mercy, compassion, forgiveness and love. Instead we replace such a God with the desire for revenge, punishment and our own definition of justice. What we have created now though is a god in our own image, a god that we can control and manipulate to meet our own needs. Is this the God we can put our faith in? Or are we, in fact, using faith in the wrong way here? It is easy, therefore, when we are angry and upset to forget the words of the Prophet Isaiah, *'For my thoughts are not your thoughts, neither are your ways my ways, declares the Lord.'* (Isaiah 55:8)

Our second book from the Old Testament, which sheds light on our search for the meaning of faith, is Job. Here we find a wealthy and prosperous man who appears to have everything in life, a wife, family, land, animals, servants, he is you might say well blessed. Then one by one he loses everything even his own health. At this point three friends question Job, who are curious, as to what he has done to deserve to be treated in such a way by God. In his response Job cannot think of anything he has done that would merit such punishment or in other words he says that he is innocent. In which case his friends claim he must be angry with God for treating an innocent man in such a way. Indeed, if Job is truly free from any guilt who, if truth be told, would blame him for being angry and for cursing God?

What, in fact, emerges from this story is the question as to why do the innocent suffer? Job is unable to work things out for himself and appeals to God. The only thing he does know is that he cannot admit to something that he has not done. What finally comes from his experience is, however, that God does not punish in a punitive way. Yet why suffering actually exists is never explained. Instead because Job refuses to condemn God all his fortunes are returned so that in the end everything is all right. What conclusions can we draw from Job then? Firstly, that suffering exists as a fact. Why it exits we just do not know and the story never explains it or attempts to. Secondly look at Job's reaction to his innocent suffering and compare it to Jonah. In Job there is no attempt born out of anger and frustration to make God do his will. Despite the fact that he continues to suffer in a terrible way Job waits, trusting in God. Equally God never abandons Job and the point being made is that God is not absent from suffering but is present in it. What is needed, however, is complete trust in God even when we suffer because he knows the end of the story even if we do not. At this point we are being granted a greater insight into the meaning of faith though it needs a little more work if we are to both understand it and appreciate it.

For a moment let us now pause and remind ourselves where we are in our journey of trying to understand the meaning of faith. We have discovered through Jesus in the parables of the *'Lost Son'* and the *'Labourers in the Vineyard'* that God is overwhelmingly generous with his love, mercy, compassion and forgiveness. However, our human nature finds this difficult to deal with hence the reaction of the eldest son and the workers who had been hired first. The Prophet Jonah also made it clear that, at least at times, we want God to act in accordance with our will rather than his. Yet the Prophet Isaiah declares that our thoughts and ways are not God's. Finally, the Book of Job draws our attention to placing all our hope and trust in God even in the midst of innocent suffering.

The next question may seem obvious but it needs to be asked, what do we put our faith in and is this more important than faith itself? To answer this question and to take our exploration further we need to turn to the *'Lord's Prayer'* and remember it was the disciples themselves who asked Jesus to teach them how to pray. Matthew's version goes like this,

'Our Father in heaven,

hallowed be your name

your kingdom come,

your will be done,

on earth as it is in heaven.

Give us this day our daily bread,

and forgive us our debts,

as we also have forgiven our debtors.

And lead us not into temptation,

but deliver us from evil.'

(Matthew 6: 9-13)

For our purposes here the key to understanding what faith actually is begins with the first line. The prayer is addressed to God the Father and later we are asking that his will be done not ours and this is exactly where the problem lies. Once again, in the parable of the *'Lost Son'* the older brother wants his Father who is, in fact God, to do his will not his Father's. In the same way in the parable of the *'Labourers in the Vineyard'* those who had been working all day want the owner, who is again God, to conform his will to theirs. In both cases there seems to be an inability to cope with the will of God, which is to be overwhelmingly generous, merciful, compassionate and forgiving to all people. Look again at the Prophet Jonah who simply refuses to believe that God can forgive and show mercy to the people of Nineveh. In the same way the Prophet Habakkuk wants God to act in accordance with his own will rather than God's.

Jesus asks for faith and trust, not in a word or in a concept or even in a belief but in him. This is the essence of faith. When we pray we are not asking for our will to be done but God's trusting that he knows what is best because he ultimately knows the end the of story and that includes our own. Even in the midst of innocent suffering as we find in the Book of Job the answer lies in placing all our hope, trust and faith in the God of mercy, compassion, forgiveness and love. We by ourselves cannot make sense out of innocent suffering; none of us can, so we are asked to put all our trust in the God who can. In essence we are saying that you Lord know, ultimately, what is best for us, even though for now we struggle to make sense out of it. Part of us, however, does want to scream out that this life is not fair, not just, simply not right but we cannot beat life or death, or pain or suffering only God can and it is in him that we are invited to place all our trust. We are now coming to the very heart of the answer to our question, *'What is faith?'*

'The apostles said to the Lord, 'Increase our faith.' The Lord replied, 'were your faith the size of a mustard seed you could say to this mulberry tree, 'Be uprooted and planted in the sea,' and it would obey you.' (Luke 17: 5-6)

Here Jesus seems to be saying that it really does not matter how much faith we have. A grain of mustard seed is indeed very small but in terms of faith is enough to uproot a sycamore tree. So when God speaks His word or reveals His will then even the tiniest willingness to believe in him will always be enough to connect us to him. What we are really saying is that, 'Lord if it is your will that a sycamore tree be uprooted then it will be, so your will be done.' However, we must never forget that this God who we are invited to place all our hope, trust and faith in is the God of mercy, compassion, forgiveness and love for all people and not just you or me. Remember Jesus in the Garden of Gethsemane on the night that he was betrayed, knowing what lay ahead of him and struggling to come to terms with the full horrors of it finally prayed, *'Nevertheless, let your will be done, not mine.'* (Luke 22:42)

At this point I was tempted to stop because I felt that I had answered the question. Then in the classroom one day a boy's hand shot up and he asked,

'How do we know any of this is true?'

I replied by asking him my own question,

'Do you pray?'

His honest response was,

'No!'

At this point I was intrigued so I asked him a further question,

'What do you like doing in your spare time?'

He thought about it and said,

'Playing on my X Box!'

'Right,' I said, *'and how long each day do you like doing that?'*

He gave it some thought and with a smile replied,

'About an hour a day!'

Suddenly a plan began to form in my mind and after a short pause I presented it to him,

'How about I play on the X box for an hour every day, if you also agree to pray for an hour? Not one hour solid, you can break it up into time slots of shall we say ten minutes and we will both do that for a week. Deal or not deal?'

The young man clearly thought about it before shaking his head and saying,

'Sorry but no deal!'

Why am I telling you this as part of my answer to the question, ***'What is faith?'*** The answer is quite simple, unless we are willing to invest time in developing our relationship with God how can we ever claim to know anything of his will? Remember what Jesus said, ***'Were your faith the size of a mustard seed,'*** that is all that is needed, a tiny seed of faith, a willingness to place our hope and trust not in our will but his. This does require some work on our part, whether that be prayer, reading the Bible, receiving the sacraments, caring for others or trying to live according to the mercy, compassion, forgives and love of God as revealed by Jesus. Saint Paul puts it like this, ***'Fan into a flame the gift that God gave you.'*** (Timothy 1:6) Unless we do this then, unless we are prepared to make the effort, we will always run the risk of confusing our own will with that of God's.

So I will finish my answer to the question, **'What is faith?'** with this short story. See what you think.

There was once a man running in the mountains when suddenly he slipped and fell over the edge of a cliff. Falling to a certain death and out of sheer desperation he put out a hand and somehow managed to grab hold of a branch and there he hung suspended between earth and sky. Now he would not have described himself as a religious man but, perhaps, for the first time in his life he actually prayed,

'God if you are out there and can hear me, I am asking you to save my life! If you do this I promise you in return that I will pray, read the Bible, go to church and do whatever I can to help people in need. Only please help me!'

There was of course no reply only the wind and the creaking of the branch as it threated to snap any minute. Then all of a sudden a voice said,

'Very well, I will help you.'

The man was so surprised he almost let go of the branch.

'Is that you God? He asked.

'Why of course, who else would it be?'

'And you will help me?'

'I will but you must do something for me first.'

'Anything, you just name it and I'll do it!'

'Very well then, let go of the branch.'

Thinking back now to the disciples I cannot help but wonder if they really understood what they were asking when they said to Jesus, **'Increase our faith.'** Did they know then that it would literally mean leaving everything behind to follow him? Did they know then that it would mean directly sharing in his ministry of making known the God of overwhelming mercy, compassion, forgiveness and love? Did they know then that it would mean taking up their own cross, daily, to follow him? Did they know then that they would lose their own life only to find it? Did they know then that the Father revealed by Jesus was the Father of all people including everyone and excluding no one? Finally, did they know then that their discipleship would cost them everything? If we now know these things would we dare to ask the Lord, *'Increase our faith?'*

Saint Francis of Assisi learned the cost of discipleship, his old self; he knew had to literally die if he was to become an authentic witness to Christ. He would take the words of the Gospel literally and apply them to himself, **'Sell everything you own, give the money to the poor and you will have treasure in heaven; then come follow me.'** (Luke 18:22) In response to conforming his life to that of Christ and living a life of faith, in accordance with the will of God, Francis wrote a remarkable prayer. I will finish this chapter with the words he wrote as a way of asking ourselves how authentically we are living out our own lives of faith in the world today. May God bless you now and always and may you live your life in the knowledge that no matter what happens, no matter what you go through the God of mercy, compassion, forgiveness and love as revealed by his Son, Jesus Christ will always be with you.

Prayer of Saint Francis of Assisi

Lord make me an instrument of your peace,

Where there is hatred let me sow love.
Where there is injury, pardon.
Where there is doubt, faith.
Where there is despair, hope.
Where there is darkness, light.
And where there is sadness, joy.

O divine master grant that I may
not so much seek to be consoled as to console;
to be understood as to understand;
To be loved as to love
For it is in giving that we receive and it's in pardoning that we are
pardoned.
And it's in dying that we are born to eternal life.
Amen.

'Everything is possible for the one who has faith.'

(Mark 9:24)

CHAPTER SIX

'What is a Christian?'

'My little children, I shall not be with you much longer. I give you a new commandment: love one another; just as I have loved you, you also must love one another. By this love you have for one another, everyone will know that you are my disciples.' (John 13: 33-35)

To answer this question I begin by making two points the answers to which are dependent upon each other. Firstly, to be a Christian you need to believe, as far as possible, that Jesus Christ is the Son of God. Secondly, this belief must impact on the way in which you live your life. These two points go hand in hand, and I believe, it is important that we ask ourselves questions, that we have the courage to challenge ourselves, even or indeed, especially, when it comes to matters of faith. However, my role here is to answer the question, *'What is a Christian?'* So where do I begin? Many people are surprised to find out that Jesus himself was not a Christian, he was, in fact a Jew. He was born a Jew, brought up as a Jew, lived his life as a Jew and died as a Jew. Indeed, in the early days of Christianity followers of Jesus were not referred to as Christians but as followers of *'The Way.'* It was only later at a place called Antioch that followers of Jesus began to be called Christians because they believed he was the Christ, a Greek title translated from the Hebrew word Messiah meaning the chosen or anointed one of God. Still today followers of Jesus are most often referred to as Christians. So let us get back to the question, *'What is a Christian?'*

Here I am going to let Jesus himself answer this question for me. This is not meant to be a *'cop out'* and I will have a role to play but it is important that we allow God to be God. In essence only God can really answer this question and our role is to listen and to respond. So here then are my thoughts, see what you think.

In the reading above Jesus gives his disciples something new, something that has never been said before, a new commandment, *'Love one another; just as I have loved you, you also must love one another.'* In other words Jesus himself tells his disciples and in turn us what it means to be a follower of his. In all likelihood the disciples did not understand what Jesus was saying or what he meant, that would come later. So is it possible for us to now understand what Jesus meant by these words and how they might impact on what it means to be a follower of his today? At this point we have a problem and we probably do not even know what that problem is. Well the problem is with the word *'love.'* In English we only have one word for love. So we might say *'I love chocolate or I love football or I love dogs,'* but then we might go on to say *'I love my wife or I love my children or I love my family.'* Now are we really saying that *'I love cake in the same way that I love my children?'* clearly not. So we have a linguistic problem with the word *'love'* in the English language. What makes it even worse is that in modern times we have taken the word love and trivialised it. So we might say, *'luv U'* at the end of a text, email or Instagram message. We might say, *'luv U'* at the end of a telephone conversation or in parting from someone that we hardly know or have just met! Is this really what Jesus meant when he said to his disciples, **'Love one another, just as I have loved you, you also must love one another.'** Perhaps we have become so familiar with the word that we use it too often or too casually without thinking about what we really mean. Or, perhaps, we just cannot come up with a more suitable alternative. In the same way if we are over familiar with these words of Jesus we make an assumption that we think we know what they mean when in essence we do not. Yet my contention here is, only if we can understand what these words mean to the point that they actually impact on the way in which we live our lives, will we ever be able to come anywhere near answering the question, **'What is Christian?'**

Our starting point needs to be with the text itself and the key word, **love**. The New Testament was originally written in Greek in which there are, in fact, several different words for love. Jesus himself used the word *'**Agape**,'* the highest form of love, for which people would be willing to do absolutely anything for the other, even to the point of giving up their own life. Within the early Church this was considered to be the love that originated from God and was revealed through Jesus as the expression of God's love for humanity. Jesus therefore was inviting his disciples to participate in nothing less than God's love through the self-same love that they were to have for each other. But we are left with the question, what does this actually mean in practice? How does it impact on the life of Christians today? And if the disciples of Jesus at the time did not understand it, how can we? Well remember what I said, understanding for the disciples would come later. For now they heard the words of Jesus but they could not translate them into action. Jesus knew this so he would have to show them what he meant. In other words they and in turn, us too, would have to see in the actions of Jesus what he actually meant in those words of the new commandment, *'Love one another, just as I have loved you, you also must love one another.'*

Our starting point is John's Gospel, just after the last supper. Jesus takes a basin of water and a towel and washes the feet of his disciples. They, of course, do not understand what he is doing. His actions are those of the lowest bond slave and yet he is their Lord and teacher. Not only did the disciples of Jesus find his actions incomprehensible but also offensive. Jesus then says, *'If I do not wash you, you can have nothing in common with me.'* (John 13:8) Finally, having washed all their feet Jesus went on to say, *'If I then, the Lord and Master, have washed your feet, you should wash each other's feet. I have given you an example, so that you may copy what I have done to you.'* (John 13: 14-150) Now, of course, the disciples did not need their feet washing. This was not the point of Jesus' action at all. Through washing their feet Jesus was revealing **agape**, God's love. In other words there was nothing Jesus and therefore God was not prepared to do for them. He would literally get down on his knees and wash their feet as a sign and a symbol of God's love but it was much more than that. For it was an insight into the very essence and being of God, a God who is the origin of **agape – love**. The disciples needed to see this in action; they needed to understand the implications of what Jesus was doing. That he was inviting them to participate through their own lives in the love of God as revealed in His Son, Jesus Christ, *'If I then, the Lord and Master, have washed your feet, you should wash each other's feet. I have given you an example, so that you may copy what I have done to you.'* In other words it was an invitation to love like God that, in essence, was what being a disciple of Jesus actually meant. If we can grasp that, then we are beginning to understand what it means to be a Christian. However, Jesus from this point on would draw his disciples and all those who would follow him into a deeper and deeper understanding of what this meant through following a God who revealed himself through the love-filled, self-emptying life of His Son.

Later that night Jesus was to be betrayed by one of his own disciples, a man he had chosen himself to be part of his mission to make God known. Judas Iscariot would identify Jesus to the authorities for thirty pieces of silver, the equivalent of a year's wages, the price of a slave or compensation for accidentally killing a servant. The betrayal takes place at night, with a kiss, in the garden of Gethsemane. Despite this act of betrayal Jesus and therefore God never stopped loving Judas.

Simon later called Peter, meaning rock, by Jesus because he would be the one upon whose faith the church would be built denies ever having known him three times. Jesus tells his disciples that he will be handed over to sinful men and eventually put to death. Peter's initial response is that he will go with him but Jesus tells Peter that this very night, before the cock crows he will deny ever having known him three times. Peter declares that even though the rest may deny him he never will. Subsequently when Jesus is arrested in the Garden of Gethsemane all the disciples eventually run away leaving Jesus alone to be taken by the guards. As Jesus is led away

Peter follows at a distance. When Jesus is taken into the palace of Caiaphas, the high priest, Peter enters the courtyard and begins to warm himself by the side of a charcoal fire. It is then that he is challenged three times that he knows and is therefore a disciple of Jesus. Three times, in response, Peter denies this before finally saying, *'I tell you, I have never even met the man!'* (John 18:25-27) At which point the cockcrows, Peter remembers the words of Jesus and their eyes meet across the courtyard. Despite this act of denial Jesus and therefore God never stopped loving Peter.

His own religious leaders, chief among whom is Caiaphas, the high priest, question Jesus. False witnesses are brought before the assembled court with fabricated testimony about what he is alleged to have said and done. On more than one occasion the temple guards slap Jesus but for the most part he remains silent. No one stands up for him or speaks in his defence; he is alone, abandoned by even his closet friends. Despite all the false accusations brought against him Jesus and therefore God never stops loving.

Jesus is now brought before Pontius Pilate the Roman governor of Judea and the representative of Caesar in Rome, emperor of the empire, the most powerful man in the world. Pilate tells Jesus he has the power to put him to death but decides to have him flogged instead, perhaps to teach him a lesson. Jesus is now led outside and stripped. Roman soldiers would use a *'flagrum,'* a wooden stick with leather strips attached into which were sown sharpened pieces of metal or bone. Jesus was struck thirty nine times with this instrument of torture. The idea was not to kill the person but to make them suffer as much as possible as a suitable punishment and therefore not to challenge the might of Rome again. At the end of the scourging Jesus would have been weak because of the blood loss and the pain which would have been unbearable, as a result he would have struggled to stand up let alone walk. At this point the Roman soldiers placed a crown of thorns on his head, thrust a reed into his hands and covered him with one of their cloaks. Some of the guards then punched him asking him to prophecy as to which one of them did it. Finally they knelt down in front of him and uttered the mocking refrain, *'Hail King of the Jews.'* (Matthew 27:29) Jesus however, remained silent. Pilate now makes a decision to let the crowed decide the fate of Jesus. He parades before them two men, Barabbas a murderer and a brigand and Jesus who he calls *'King of the Jews.'* (Matthew 27:22) He then asks the crowd whom they want him to release in honour of their celebration of the Passover festival. They respond immediately by shouting for '*Barabbas*!' (Matthew 27:21) Pilate then asks what he is to do with Jesus and the crowd respond by shouting *'Crucify him!'* (Matthew 27:22) Pilate now directs the soldiers to take him away and put him to death. Throughout the whole ordeal Jesus remains silent. Despite the acts of hatred and violence directed against him Jesus and therefore God never stops loving.

As he has lost so much blood, Jesus struggles to carry, by himself, the wooden horizontal beam he is to be crucified to. Instead a man from the crowd called Simon of Cyrene carries the cross to a place called Golgotha, the skull. At this point the efficiency of the Roman soldiers would have taken over. After all, to them, this was just another job, like any other routine crucifixion they had been ordered to carry out. Firstly, Jesus would have been stripped naked to maximise his humiliation. Then nails would have been hammered into his wrists, the only part of the body strong enough to hold it up, before the feet were also nailed to the vertical part of the bream. Jesus would then have been hoisted into the air for all to look upon and see. The objective was not to kill the person straight away but for them to die a slow, agonizing death as an example to all those who, in any way, questioned the authority of Rome. Those who stood by including the religious leaders taunted and mocked him, *'He saved others, let him save himself, if he is the Messiah of God.'* (Luke 23:35) Jesus, however, continued to remain silent. Those who were crucified could take days to die and that, at least in part, was the intention. However, Jesus was weak, he had been up all-night and flogged to the point of near exhaustion. His body therefore could not take much more and in the end he gave up his spirit and died. Despite the cruelty of his death Jesus and therefore God never stopped loving.

It is time now to go back to where we started with Jesus and his disciples, *'Love one another, just as I have loved you, you also must love one another.'* When Jesus said those words to his disciples they, of course, did not know what he really meant, understanding would come later; Jesus would, however, have to show them its full depth. From the foot washing in the upper room to his death on the cross Jesus would literally reveal to them what God's love was like. It was this love that Jesus was inviting them to participate in as his followers. He also went on to say to them, *'By this love you have for one another, everyone will know that you are my disciples.'* The meaning of Jesus's words now become plain, others will recognise his followers by the love they have for each other. However, that love is called *'agape'* and it cost Jesus ultimately his life but in so doing revealed the love of God for everyone. This allows us now to go back to our original question, *'What is a Christian?'* A Christian is someone who believes, as far as possible, that Jesus Christ is the Son of God and allows that belief to impact on the way in which they live their lives. Jesus, himself, tells us that to follow him means to live a life of love (agape) and in his life he reveals both the depth and the meaning of that love whose origin, itself, is God. Imagine what life would be like if we could really live like that. Lives literally dedicated to the service and love of each other, modelled on the life of Jesus but actually participating in the life of God who himself is love. Our homes, places of work, parishes and communities would be transformed. A church that fights amongst itself or who tells people to do one thing but does the opposite itself does not attract people. But a loved filled community dedicated to justice, integrity and the well-being and the welfare of others is attractive. For there we can see before our very eyes the face of God in Christ himself. The Christian is someone who believes they are called by Christ to live a life according to his commandment *'to love one another in the same way as I have loved you.'* Jesus himself shows us, literally, what this means. It cost him his life and there will be a cost to being one of his disciples too but God's love is already there waiting and inviting us just to participate in it and when we accept that invitation everything changes and our lives our transformed. Moreover, if Christians love one another with the same love with which Jesus loved them, they will literally experience his presence with them. To love like that is the vocation of every Christian because it is through the love they have for each other that Jesus, who is himself love, will continue to spread among them. In this way the words of Jesus are realised or sacramentally made present because, *'By this love you have for one another, everyone will know that you are my disciples.'* Such love does nothing less than define the identity of every Christian because it is true to the spirit of Jesus realised in their lives. Love then, that is to say self-sacrificial *'agape'* love is **the** distinguishing feature of Christian identity and it is here that ultimately we find the answer to our question, *'What is a Christian?'* But, of course, unless this is lived or actually incarnated in our lives it remains an academic or theoretical exercise. However, Jesus, as we have seen shows us the way, all we have to do now is follow him and the example he set whilst keeping in our hearts his words and knowing that he is with us always, even unto the end of time. (Matthew 28:20)

CHAPTER SEVEN

'What is the Trinity and how can it help me in life?'

'I have much more to say to you, more than you can bear. But when he, the Spirit of truth, comes, he will guide you into all truth. He will not speak on his own; he will speak only what he hears, and he will tell you what is to come. He will bring glory to me by taking from what is mine and making it known to you. All that belongs to the Father is mine. That is why I said the Spirit will take from what is mine and make it known to you. In a little while you will see me no more and then after a little while you will see me.' (John 16:12-15)

'The Father and I are one (John 10:30)

What a question this is. I remember once going into a church in Yorkshire on a boiling hot sunny evening in June. It was one of those really hot oppressive days with little or no breeze and the church felt like it had been shut all day trapping the heat inside. It was Trinity Sunday and when it came to the homily, the priest got straight to the point, *'I spent six months studying the Trinity at seminary. I didn't understand it then and I don't understand it now! What's more it's too hot to preach!'* and with that he stopped and simply moved on to the next part of the mass.

Now in one sense the priest was completely right, in so far as, the Trinity is a mystery. So let us at this moment pause and briefly summarise what Trinity means. Most Christians believe that the one God, reveals himself in three different ways that is to say as God the Father, God the Son (Jesus) and God the Holy Spirit. They are often referred to as the three persons of the Trinity. Once this has been established we can then go on to say that they are equal to each other, can never be parted or separated from one another and are bound together by love. However, this in itself raises a whole load of different other questions starting with, *'What does this actually mean?'* Well the simple truth is that theologians have for millennia tried to explain the meaning of the Trinity. '*Why?*' you might ask. Well the simple and at the same time complex answer is so that we may know and experience the mystery of God more intimately. For this reason, formulas, concepts, images, diagrams, pictures, paintings, models and explanations have all been put forward to explain to what amounts to God's relationship with himself. There is nothing wrong with that because it reflects a deep desire within humanity to know God better. However, does it help answer our question and the answer has to be, no! So we need some help if we are ever to get to grips with the question, '***How can the Trinity help me in life?***'

Thankfully we can turn, once again, to Jesus, for help. Jesus can, of course, reflect on his own relationship with His Father to shed light on whom and what God actually is. First and foremost Jesus invites us to refer to God as Father, *'So you should pray like this: 'Our Father in Heaven,'* (Matthew 6:9) At the same time Jesus also invites us to be led by him, as the Son of God, whilst at the same time being inspired by the Holy Spirit. In other words Jesus encourages an openness to God, who though mystery, can be understood if we allow ourselves to be guided by grace.

If we are to relate to God as Father then Jesus also encourages us to see ourselves as His children. Here we note the words of Jesus to his disciples when he says, *'My little children, I shall not be with you much longer.'* (John 13:33) In this way, it would seem, Jesus is telling us to see God the Father not as being distant and unknown but as close and accessible. This image also portrays God the Father not in terms of power, might and control but instead as being about mercy, compassion, forgiveness and above all love. As a result, no one is ever truly alone but rather Jesus reveals a loving Father who is closer to us than we could ever imagine; one who understands everything about us because he loves us and forgives us and desires us to know that he cares for us in a way that no one else ever could. This is the Trinity alive and active in our lives drawing us deeper and deeper into God himself. This is what Jesus wants us to know, understand and experience and it is this that will help us see just how the Trinity can help us every single day of our lives.

Jesus also reveals something that flows out of the Father's heart, a desire to establish his Kingdom. Hence returning to the Lord's Prayer we find, *'Your kingdom come.'* (Matthew 6:9) But what exactly does this mean?

First and foremost this kingdom is born out of nothing apart from his love and we, as his children, are invited to build it with him. This, however, is unlike any kingdom that has ever existed before because fundamentally it is inclusive, no one is excluded from the Kingdom of God. This is about building a more just world for everyone, guaranteeing dignity to all but beginning with those who are most weak, most vulnerable and those who are most powerless. Jesus invites all of us to be part of building up this kingdom, which belongs to the Father; we are led there by the Son and inspired by the Holy Spirit. Once again, if we do this we, are in fact, living the Trinity by reaching out to everyone and excluding no one.

However, if we are ever going to achieve this there is one thing that Jesus insists on and that is, that we must place all our hope and all our trust in him, *'Do not let your hearts be troubled. Trust in God still and trust in me.'* (John 14:1) Fundamental to an understanding of the Trinity is that Jesus is nothing less than the Son of God, the second person of the Trinity and that he shares directly and equally in the life of the one God. Now the words of Jesus in the Gospel of John make complete sense, *'The Father and I are one.'* (John 10: 30) Therefore through the words and the actions of Jesus we see God and most importantly of all know, believe and understand that he unconditionally loves each and every single one of us, no one is excluded. So, and as a result of this, Jesus invites us to follow him and by him and through him learn how to place all our trust and all our hope in the Father, just like he did. We are invited therefore to be servants of the Kingdom of God following Jesus's commandment to, *'Love one another, just as I have loved you; you also must love one another.'* (John 13:34) Our vocation, then, is to reflect the nature and being of God who is of himself, mercy, compassion, forgiveness and love. If we follow Jesus he will teach us how to put all our trust in the Father, how to be gentle, kind and understanding and how, therefore, to participate in the very life of God himself who is by his very nature Trinity.

As we follow in the footsteps of Jesus then something new happens, a new community is formed, reflecting a new way of living, a new way of being. The task of this new community is to do the Father's will, *'Your will be done, on earth as in heaven.'* (Matthew 6:10) Eventually Jesus will leave this new community on earth as he ascends to be with the Father, in heaven. This new community we call the church and its primary task is to incarnate, make visibly present, the continuing work of Jesus to make the Kingdom of God alive and active in the here and now. Just as Jesus went out in search of the poorest and most vulnerable people of his time, those who believed themselves to be rejected, despised, unwanted and unloved, even by God, so the church must do the same and assure all people of God's unconditional love today. If this new community can do this it will become an authentic sign and symbol of what it is called to represent, that is God, *'By this love you have for one another, everyone will know that you are my disciples.'* (John 13:35) When this happens people will be able to see right before their very eyes, that something new is being established, something new is being created that has never existed before, which is not a reflection of the will of man but of the will of God. This is the kind of world that God the Father desires and invites us to participate in. Again to do so means to live the life of the Trinity itself.

However, none of this can happen unless our lives are set on fire by the gift of the Holy Spirit, the third person of the Trinity, when that happens Jesus assures us that we can do anything in His name, *'You will receive power when the Holy spirit comes upon you and you will be my witnesses.'* (Acts 1:8) And what a gift this is! The Holy Spirit is nothing less than the Spirit of love that binds together the Father and the Son and it is this self-same spirit that Jesus tells us is poured out into our own hearts. Only the Holy Spirit shared by the Father and the Son can give us the strength and the faith to do the Father's will in the here and now of our lives. Only the Holy Spirit can give us the will, the drive and the energy to enable us to be authentic witnesses to Jesus Christ, the Son of God. Only the Holy Spirit will enable us to work tirelessly and ceaselessly to establish the Kingdom of the Father here on earth, which is a reflection of his will for all people. A Kingdom in which everyone is welcome and no one is excluded but a Kingdom like no other because it is founded on the nature and being of the Father who of himself and by his very essence is mercy, compassion, forgiveness and love. Jesus invites us to participate in this life of God in the here and now and when we accept this invitation, when we become witnesses to him, when we point to him, when we work to establish the Father's Kingdom enlivened by the Holy Spirit, then our very lives become nothing less than reflections of the Trinitarian God.

CHAPTER EIGHT

'Is Jesus God?'

'I am the Way and the Truth and the Life' (John 14:6)

What a question this is! It is one though that, very often, many people misunderstand and get confused over. So for the purposes of this chapter and in response to the question, I am going to focus my answer on the Gospel of John and what Jesus actually says about himself there. In John's Gospel one of the central themes is the way in which Jesus is portrayed as being the unique representation of God to the human race. Focusing attention on one phrase, which Jesus took from the Old Testament and controversially applied exclusively to himself, does this. At first this phrase will sound strange to the reader but as we delve deeper into its origins the mystery of Jesus's true identity will be revealed. The phrase I am talking about is, *'I am'* or *'It is I'*, in Greek, the original language of the New Testament, it is expressed as 'Εγώ ειμ.' Before we can explain fully the implications of this, however, we need to pause and be a little bit technical I'm afraid! In Hebrew, the original language of the Old Testament, God is given a name which contains four letters (יהוה in Hebrew, and YHWH in Latin), meaning *'I am that I am'* or *'I will be what I will be,'* something often referred to as tetragrammaton because of its use of four letters. At this stage we will just note the link between the title given to Jesus in John's Gospel and the name of God in the Hebrew Scriptures, commonly called the Old Testament but this link will be vital to our claims about who Jesus actually is and therefore our answer to the original question.

John throughout his Gospel goes to great lengths to stress that Jesus is the only one who has true life in himself and that he has come that others may share in that life, by participating in the eternal fellowship of God. As a result Jesus is able to say, *'I came that they may have life, and have it abundantly.'* (John 10:10) However, everything in John and his understanding of who Jesus actually is hinges on his use of the *'I am'* titles and their link to the first use of God's name on Mount Horeb in the book of Exodus, *'God said to Moses, "I am who I am." He said further, "Thus you shall say to the Israelites, "I am has sent me to you."'* (Exodus 3:13) Here it is important to note the fact that this expression evokes the name of God by association, even if it does not itself represent the name. However, what we can say is clear, that these words more than, perhaps, any other in the whole of the New Testament provide the foundation for understanding who Jesus actually is. For John the use of the title, *'I am'* means nothing less than he is, in fact, God. Jews, of course, avoid using the name of God at all as it is deemed to be too holy but John has no hesitation in reaching deep into the Hebrew Scriptures to make the direct connection between Jesus and God. Therefore, for John, it is obvious that every time Jesus uses the title *'I am,'* he is, in effect, declaring openly and before all people that he is nothing less than God.

When we compare the use of the *'I am'* title in the synoptic gospels, the first three (Matthew, Mark and Luke), to that of John we find that the latter uses it thirty more times. Equally the synoptic gospels suggest that Jesus grew gradually in his knowledge and understanding of who he was, whilst John makes the point, consistently, that Jesus knew all along his true divine identity. John the Baptist is used by John in a negative way stating clearly and openly who he is not so that any confusion as to who he might be is removed, *'Who are you?' he not only declared, but he declared quite openly, I am not the Christ.'* (John 1: 20-21) In this way Jesus's unique importance and identity is highlighted as the core of the gospel message, his and no one else. Adding to this John also makes it clear that unlike the Hebrew prophets of old Jesus is not simply delivering a received message from outside of himself. No, and instead, he teaches as one with authority in and of himself, *'If anyone hears my words and does not keep them faithfully,'* (John 12:47). Going on from this Jesus also uses the *'I am'* titles no less than seven times, a perfect number for the Jews, and perfection can only be found in God. Equally every time he uses the statement it is linked directly and without any ambiguity to central images of the Jewish faith and law, which in turn are now being fulfilled in Jesus. In this way John is clearly painting a picture of Jesus as God who though he exists outside of time has chosen now to enter it. For example when Jesus says, *'I am the light of the world'* (John 8:12) we can see a clear link to, *'Arise shine, for your light has come'* in Isaiah 60:1 or when Jesus says *'I am the good shepherd'* (John 10:14) we can understand this as a fulfilment of, *'I myself will be the shepherd of my sheep,'* from Ezekiel 34:15. The same could equally be said for Jesus's description of himself as bread, the vine, the way, the truth and the life. John consistently is making it clear that Jesus not only fulfils the Hebrew Scriptures he does so as God in the here and now.

It is time now to go back to the beginning of John's Gospel because right from the start he makes an unambiguous statement about who Jesus actually is, *'In the beginning was the word, and the word was with God, and the word was God.'* (John 1:1) For John Jesus is the 'word' of God present at the beginning of everything and made flesh in him through the incarnation, *'The word was made flesh, he lived among us, and we saw his glory, the glory that is his as the only Son of the Father, full of grace and truth.'* (John 1:14) In this way John is making a direct link with the opening words of the Bible, *'In the beginning God created the heavens and the earth.'* (Genesis 1:1) In other words this Jesus who became one of us is also the God who in the beginning created everything. When we put this together with the *'I am'* statements Jesus's answer to the question asked of him by the Jews becomes abundantly clear, *'You are not yet fitty years old, and have seen Abraham?'* Jesus replied, *'I tell you most solemnly before Abraham ever was, I AM.'* (John 8:57-58) Such statements identify Jesus with the name for God mentioned in the Hebrew Scriptures by asserting who God is; nothing less than the one named in the tetragrammaton, is the same God who proclaims himself uniquely in the *'I am'* sayings.

When we examine the *'I am'* sayings in more detail what we find is almost a set formula in operation, one which applies the Old Testament and the Jews understanding of God to Jesus, who in his person, embodies and fulfils them. We can see this illustrated perfectly in the following example, *'I tell you most solemnly, it was not Moses who gave you bread form heaven, it is my Father who gives you the bread from heaven, the true bread; for the bread of God is that which comes down from heaven and gives life to the world.' 'Sir they said 'give us this bread always.' Jesus answered, 'I am the bread of life. He comes to me will never be hungry, he who believes in me will never thirst.'* (John 6:32-36) In this way Jesus is saying that he is the true bread of life and that the life that he offers comes directly from God and is, therefore, eternal.

In the same way Jesus is the light of the world, *'As long as I am in the world, I am the light of the world.'* (John 9:5) Here we see a direct link to chapter one of John where he says, *'The word was the true light that enlightens all men; and he was coming into the world.'* John 1: 9) Now Jesus is the light, issuing from the source of all light that gives life to people. So as we delve deeper into John and the identity of Jesus as God we come across his claims to exclusivity. He and He alone is the door of the sheep pen and therefore the only way to the Father. It is only through him that pastors can perform their ministry and the sheep must come into the Church through the only accessible door, which is Jesus himself, *'I am the good shepherd. I know my own and my own know me, just as the Father knows me and I know the Father. The Father loves me, because I lay down my life in order to take it up again. No one takes it from me, but I lay it down of my own accord. I have power to lay it down, and I have power to take it up again. I have received this command from my Father.'* (John 10:14-19) We should note here also a direct link to the resurrection of Jesus and how he will lay down his life for his sheep but will rise to new life. This is powerful stuff. But we are not finished yet, *'I am the gate. Whoever enters by me will be saved, and he will come in and go out and find pasture. The thief comes only to steal and kill and destroy. I came that they may have life, and have it abundantly. I am the good shepherd. The good shepherd lays down his life for the sheep.'*

(John 10: 9-12)

Finally we come to another critical aspect of identifying Jesus as God. It is Jesus himself who makes these claims and once again by linking his life with that of God and his relationship with his people, the Jews, in the Old Testament he makes it abundantly clear that without him people can do nothing, *'I am the vine, you are the branches. Those who abide in me and I in them bear much fruit, because apart from me you can do nothing.'* (John 15:5) In this way Jesus through his life and ministry communicates who God is and that without him there can be no existence. In this way Jesus is unique and through the *'I am'* sayings reveals his true identity. In ancient Israel the vine and its branches perfectly illustrated the relationship between God and his people. This metaphor makes it clear that without the vine, who is God, the branches, God's people the Jews, can do nothing. Then Jesus makes this amazing statement, *'I am the vine, you are the branches. Those who abide in me and I In them bear much fruit, because apart from me you can do nothing.'* (John 15:5) Finally, as if to make everything even clearer Jesus says, *'I am the way, the truth, and the life. No one comes to the Father except through me. If you know me, you will know my Father also.'* (John 14:6-8)

Some Final Thoughts

In John's Gospel and through the *'I am'* sayings Jesus declares things about himself that have never been uttered by anyone before or since in so far as he states openly that he is God incarnate, the word made flesh. In this way God enters our time and our space to reveal who He is and what that means for the human race. Having said that, although he is God in the flesh, as it were, he is not limited like we are, rather He and the Father are one and he can lay down his life and take it up again. In this sense it is not just about what Jesus does but about whom he actually is that matters most. The path to God, therefore, is through Jesus in whom the fullness of life and truth are to be found. This is what God, in and through His Son, offers us. Jesus himself is this life and I will close this chapter with the words of Jesus himself, *'This indeed is the will of my Father that all who see the Son and believe in him may have eternal life; and I will raise them up on the last day.'* (John 6:40)

CHAPTER NINE

'If Jesus came to change things, why is everything still the same?'

'Take courage it is I. Do not be afraid' (John 6: 20-21)

What a great question this is and it was asked of me by an eleven year old girl from year six in a primary school. So I am going to try and write down the answer I gave to the young lady and leave you, the reader, to decide for yourself whether it is satisfactory or not.

To answer this question my starting point is with another question, not the right approach, I know, but at least I am going to try and answer it. So here we go. *Do you think this how God intended things to be? Just look at the world in which we live from crime, poverty and injustice to war, pollution, cruelty, disease and famine; is this really how God wanted things to be?'*

The answer to this has to be clearly, *'No!'* But if this is the case, *'Why haven't things changed because of Jesus?'* To provide any kind of answer to that question, which is after all our starting point, we need to go right back to the beginning of everything.

In the book of Genesis we are told that God created all things before finally creating Adam, who represented all men and Eve who represented all women and by the way that includes you and me. He then placed them in the Garden of Eden where they would literally want for nothing. Here there would be no pain, no suffering, no war, no sickness, and no disease, not even death. In other words they would be in paradise and this is how God intended things to be for everyone. The one thing, however, God asked them not to do was to eat from the tree in the middle of the garden, the tree of knowledge, the tree of good and evil, apart from that they could literally do whatever they liked. Tempted by the devil in the form of a serpent both Adam and Eve used their free will and ate the fruit from the tree. Two things now happened; firstly they are embarrassed by their nakedness and covered themselves up and secondly when challenged by God, as to their actions, they blame each other for their misdeeds. In other words they fall into the trap of judging each other as they think they know better than God or to put it a different way they, themselves, know the difference between right and wrong without the need for God. God's response, which is to echo down through time, is simply, *'Why did you do that?'* (Genesis 3:13) When you had everything you could possibly want, why did you choose to give in to temptation? Now remember that both Adam and Eve, together, really represent the whole of humanity and this is the same question, therefore, that each and every single one of us could ask of ourselves today and possibly even every day.

We know what happens next but before we move on we need to make sure that we understand the point being made here. Humanity through Adam and Eve are really saying, *'We don't need you God because we know better than you. We can work out for ourselves the difference between right and wrong, after all that's why you've given us free will isn't it? No, we will now judge each other, we don't need you!'* This is very important because Adam and Eve now leave the Garden of Eden behind to make their own way in the world. They reject what God had originally intended for them because, putting it simply, they, in fact, knew better. Of course the very next chapter of Genesis describes how Adam and Eve, literally all men and all women, go on to have children one of whom, Cain, kills his bother Abel. This is the first recorded murder in the Bible and this is where humanities rejection of God has led them to and from now on things can only get worse.

However, God never stops loving his creation and in particular humanity made in his own image, **Genesis 1: 26**, and the call of Abraham, **Genesis 12: 1-3, 17: 1-8** makes this point abundantly clear. For God through Abraham and his descendants binds himself to them through a special relationship called a covenant. God will never break this agreement and all he asks for in return is faith, ***'and I will be your God for ever…..'*** **(Genesis 17: 7)** In very simple language God promises unconditional love to Abraham and his descendants for all time and they are asked to do, literally, nothing in return. God goes on to promise Abraham children, though he is old and a new land to live in though it is far away. All Abraham has to do is to trust God.

The rest of the first half of the Bible, in many ways, is an exploration of the ever-changing relationship between God and humanity. Time and time again humanity turns its back on God and walks, figuratively, further and further away. It is almost possible to hear the collective refrain, *'We don't need you, we don't need you!'* But God never stops loving his people and calling them back to him but they must choose to return for themselves. In this respect the wonderful story of Moses illustrates perfectly what happens when people put their trust in God, they are delivered. However, no sooner are the Hebrews delivered from slavery in Egypt than they turn on Moses fearing that he has led them out into the desert to die. The crossing of the Red Sea **(Exodus 14),** the manna from heaven (**Exodus 16**) and the water gushing from the rock *(Numbers 20)* all illustrate that God will never abandon His people. In the end God, in fact, gives them more. If they are to be faithful to him, if they are to find their way back to him then they must behave in a certain way, they cannot do it by themselves, they simply cannot continue to do what Adam and Eve symbolised on behalf of us all by saying, *'We will decide for ourselves what is right and wrong, we will be our own judges.'* So God's response is to give them a set of laws to live by, the Ten Commandments **(Exodus 20),** so that surely now they will know how to behave. If they, somehow, can keep these laws then in doing so they will be faithful to him. This then becomes one of the ways God acts, in and through time, just as he did in the story of the Exodus to call his people back to him when, in fact, they had strayed so far away.

I am going to stop at this point because it was about now that the young lady who asked the original question wanted some clarification, this is what she asked, **'Sometimes you talk about humanity, meaning everyone and sometimes you talk about the Jews as being the people of God, what do you mean by this?'** If you remember at the start I said that Adam and Eve represent everyone and they do and that includes you and me by the way. However, God also called the Jews and developed a special relationship with them called a covenant; remember Abraham? Yet the Jews were also given another mission because it would be through them that the whole of humanity would be drawn back to God. Isaiah put it like this, *'I will make you the light of the nation's so that my salvation may reach to the ends of the earth.'* **(Isaiah 49:6)** God commits himself to everyone leaving no one out and that is why we can say his love is inclusive of all people.

However, once again things started to go wrong. The Jews eventually wanted a king who could be God's representative among them but even the kings lost their way. The Law, which originally took the form of Ten Commandments, finally ended up as 613 rules many of which can be found in the book of *Leviticus* emphasizing ritual, legal and moral practices rather than belief in God. The danger now was that the Law, which was originally designed to draw people closer to God, was taking on a disproportionate importance in its own right making it impossible for some people to keep all of it. God's response is to send prophets both men and women who could speak on his behalf reminding them of what they are called to be, *'A light to the nations.'* Many of these prophets were rejected and driven out when they reminded the people what God wanted, *'Since what I want is mercy, not sacrifice; knowledge of God not holocausts.'* (Hosea 6:6) cried the prophet Hosea. When confronted with the way in which God's people, with whom he had made a covenant, had turned their backs on the poor and needy and had failed to live according to his justice the prophet Micah reminds them that this is what God wants from you, *'To act justly and to love mercy and to walk humbly with your God.'* (Micah 6:8) However, still things did not change and humanity moved further and further away from God.

Having been conquered several times by different nations including the Babylonians and the Greeks we finally enter that time in history when Rome came to power. They conquered Israel the Promised Land given to Abraham and his descendants forever, renaming it Palestine and placed their own governor in charge whilst allowing a Jew, as a puppet king, to sit on the throne. The faith of the Jews was now in serious trouble. The Pharisees emphasised the importance of keeping the Torah, the Law, of which as we have already seen there were 613 precepts. The name Pharisee actually means the separated ones and this is what they advocated for God's people, that by following His Law, they should keep themselves as separated as possible from everybody else on earth, whom they called Gentiles and that also included the Romans. So what happened to their mission to be a light to the nations you might ask?

The Sadducees another religious group belonging to the Jews focused attention on the purity of worship in God's temple in Jerusalem. The Herodian's wanted to restore Herod to the throne and not a descendant of King David like the Pharisees whilst the Zealots advocated a violent and religious rebellion against the occupying Roman forces.

In this way we can clearly see that humanity since the Garden of Eden and Adam and Eve had lost its way but was totally unaware of it. Time and time again it is possible to see the actions of Adam and Eve lived out in and through the actions of Israel and the whole of humanity, *'We don't need you, we can find our own way, we will decide right and wrong for ourselves, we will be our own judges.'* One word that I have not used so far is *sin* but perhaps this word like no other best sums up where humanity found itself at this time in history. It had rebelled against its own creator and had tried to forge a god in its own image. The distance between humanity and God had become so great it was impossible to cross, the damage so deep it was impossible to repair and the wound so damaging it was impossible to heal. So what could be done? The answer is that humanity could, in truth, do nothing by itself, even if it wanted to. Only God could bridge such a distance, only God could heal such a wound and only God could repair such damage. But to do that God would have to recreate everything and in the end pay the ultimate price, the death of His own Son.

One way of looking at and understanding Jesus is to explore the link between him and Adam. We have already established that Adam is the representative of all humanity, though not without Eve. Jesus as the second person of the Trinity, the Son of God, empties himself to become like us in every way except sin. So when Adam rejects God, to go his own way in the world, deciding his own morality and assuming the role of judge, Jesus does the opposite. Jesus conforms his will to that of his Father and will do so for the whole of his ministry but he will do this as one who is fully human whilst being also fully God in one and the same person. If things are to be put right, if the relationship between humanity and God is to be restored and healed then three things have to be dealt with:

a) Sin – the path chosen by humanity through Adam's decision to reject God

b) Satan – the power of evil in opposition to God

c) Death – the consequences of sin and the desire of Satan

However, God can only do this from the inside out and by this I mean through the flesh of the new Adam, who is Christ. At the same time there will be a terrible price or a cost for God to pay because it will result in the death of His own Son.

People often ask me how come Jesus, such a good man ended up being crucified? Firstly, let us deal with the question by stating that Jesus was not as the question puts it a good man, rather he is the Son of God, who in and of himself was fully God and fully human in one and the same person. Secondly, Jesus's death was inevitable because humanity had already chosen, as we have seen, to go its own way and that was without God. For Jesus then three things converge all aimed at destroying him, that is to say, Satan, sin and death. Sin the rejection of God by Adam, Eve and all human beings since humanity had already made its choice to abandon Him and only He could deal with this. Death, not part of God's original plan but as a direct consequence of sin brought on by our own selves which, once again, could only be dealt with by God. And finally only God could defeat Satan, compliant in the first sin and all those committed ever since, who wills not only our death but also that of God in Christ too.

What happens next involves transformation of everything, a recreation of the universe, akin to that at the beginning as described in **Genesis**. The sin of humanity represented in the first instance by Adam and Eve puts Jesus on the cross. Why crucifixion? In the book of **Deuteronomy 21:23** we are told that the man who hangs on a tree is *'cursed'* by God something Saint Paul himself quotes in **Galatians 3: 10-14**. In other words there can be no greater shame for a Jew than to die on a tree. When we add to this the fact that Jesus is crucified outside the walls of Jerusalem, the holy city, we are beginning to get the impression that Jesus is not only being abandoned by

God but that his death has consequences for everyone, the whole of humanity. Crucifixion is a brutal way to die but when we keep in mind the fact that Jesus was scourged beforehand and as with all those sentenced to die in this way he would have been naked and therefore shamed for all to see, his death takes on a new significance. In him, on that cross we see the consequences of sin and just how far humanity had fallen since the first sin of Adam. In him on that cross we also see the desire of Satan, the same desire that was present in the Garden of Eden to see the destruction of humanity and its relationship with God. If God in and through His Son is to transform and recreate everything then he must as the new or second Adam take all that sin into himself and still remain faithful to the Father's will. Everything must be changed from the inside out and that includes experiencing the absence of God, hence we have the cry of Jesus as he nears the end of his life, *'My God, My God, why have you forsaken me.'* (Matthew 27:46 and Psalm 22:2) What is true is that Jesus has in his life relived the life of Adam and God's people in their entirety the only difference being that he remained faithful to the Father's will right up to and including the end. Only in this way could he ever be a true representative of the human race.

At this point we really need to stop and think hard about what we are truly saying. To look upon Jesus on that cross must have been a terrible sight to behold, from the nails through the wrists and feet, to the lacerations from the scourging and the crown of thorns; we cannot help but think of the words from the prophet Isaiah, *'He was wounded for our transgressions, he was bruised for our iniquities; upon him was the chastisement that made us whole, and with his stripes we are healed.'* (Isaiah 53:5) Yet this is exactly the point because in and through the life of Jesus, as the new Adam, the whole history of Israel is relived to the point that the sin of humanity and therefore of us all is taken into him. Once again Isaiah says, *'We had all gone astray like sheep, and the Lord brought the acts of rebellion of all of us to bear on him.'* (Isaiah 53:6) Going on he continues, *'Like a lamb led to the slaughter house, like a sheep dumb before its shearers he never opened his mouth.'* (Isaiah 53:7) Finally, we come across the telling words, *'… at his having been cut off from the land of the living, at his having been struck dead for his people's rebellion.'* (Isaiah 53:8) And yet these are the actions of God, *the crucified God*, and the God who comes to do for us what were incapable of doing for ourselves; that is to say free us from sin. But to do this there must also be death, so that God in and through His Son can also share the true price of sin and its ultimate cost, that to which we have been bound since the first Adam's rejection; namely the grave, *'Jesus cried out in a loud voice saying, Father, into your hands I commend my spirit. With these words he breathed his last.'* (Luke 23:46) It would seem now, therefore, and for the entire world to see, that Satan, sin and death had all won and that God in Christ had, in fact, been defeated but what follows next changes everything.

Three days later, the resurrection transforms and recreates creation itself and there is now a new beginning; things can start all over again. The powers of this world, Satan, sin and death, have all been defeated and the relationship between God and humanity has been repaired and restored. Now everything has changed and nothing can ever be the same again, sin and Satan have lost their hold on the human race and death has been destroyed forever. In this way God has, in effect, rewritten creation in and through his own flesh. In one sense and because of Adam but before the resurrection we were all dead but now in Christ we are all truly alive. Though we were the ones who Crucified God, this same Crucified God now shares his very life with us. But more than that, this Crucified God actually allows us to participate fully in his life. Now we are really coming to the point of answering the initial question, *'If Jesus came to change things, why is everything still the same?'* The answer is that nothing is the same, in fact everything has changed it is just that most of us do not realise it but that does not change the reality of its truth. The Crucified God has destroyed sin, defeated Satan and vanquished death forever. Hence the first words of Jesus to the women after his resurrection from the dead were, *'Do not be afraid,'* (Matthew 28: 10) to reassure them that everything had changed and nothing would ever be the same again. For in truth the Crucified God has rewritten the story of humanity and we can and do participate directly in this new life now. For God did not come to make people good but to give life to the dead. Within each and every single one of us is the victory of the Crucified God. Next time we are tempted to act or behave in a way that is contrary to this act of supreme love we need to reach deep within ourselves and find something better. There is nothing we can do because it has already been done; the love of the Crucified God has triumphed over everything defeating sin, Satan and death forever. This is the truth of the Christian faith. The Sacraments of the Church make this a living reality because each of them allows us to experience the love of the Crucified God in a physical way, here and now.

Through Baptism we die with Christ only to rise with him to a new life that not even death can take away from us. The sacrament of reconciliation allows us to experience the mercy and forgiveness of God in the here and now. Holy Communion is nothing less than a participation in the life of God through reception of His real body and His real blood. Confirmation confirms the grace given to us at baptism and is a calling to go out and bear witness to the God of love in the world knowing that He is always present with us and never absent. Marriage is a sharing in the unconditional love that exists within the heart of God as Father, Son and Holy Spirit, whilst at the same time being a call to reflect that love in the world. Ordination is an invitation from God in Christ to know him, serve him and love him through a life dedicated to the love and service of others. Finally, the anointing of the sick is a confirmation that there is no part of our experience that God is absent from and that includes our pain and suffering as well as our death.

All of this is achieved and is only possible through the Crucified God, who in Jesus said, *'I have come that you may have life and have it to the full.'* (John 10:10)

CHAPTER TEN

'When I am going through a hard time can you tell me three things about Jesus that might help me?'

'Simon son of John, do you love me?' He replied, 'Yes Lord you know I

love you.' (John 21:16)

The Three Gifts of Jesus

To answer this question I am going to talk about and offer what I call the three gifts of Jesus. So for anybody going through a hard time in life, no matter what it is from a bereavement, to the diagnosis of a terminal illness, from domestic violence to debt and everything else in between I invite you to reflect upon each of these gifts given to us by God, himself, through His Son Jesus Christ.

The Gift of Love

'I give you a new commandment love one another just as I have loved you, you also must love one another.' (John 13: 34-35)

Imagine, if you will, being seen by Jesus and being told by him that *'He loves you,'* and by that I mean, you. Not the person next to you or the person that you know who you feel is better than you are, not a saint but you. Of course you might react by saying that you are not worthy of such love but that applies to all of us without exception. So, you cannot opt out of this, Jesus will not let you go. He has loved you and I mean you and uniquely you since before you were born. In fact he has loved you, he does love you and he will continue to love you for all time. But you might say again, *'I've done terrible things!'* That does not change the fact that he still loves you. However, you are trying to resist it by saying to yourself, *'Who could possibly love me like that?'* Well what about the tax collector, Matthew (Matthew 9: 9-13), hated by everyone because he cheated people out of their money, Jesus still chose him to be a disciple. Then what about Peter whom Jesus chose to be the leader of the disciples and yet it was him who denied ever having known Jesus three times. (Luke22: 54-62) Then what about Judas Iscariot who betrayed Jesus? (Matthew 26:15) What about the woman caught in the act of committing adultery? (John 8: 1-11) Need I go on? The list is in fact endless. You see the nature and the being of God as revealed in Jesus is simply to love, to continue to love, to never stop loving and to give that unconditional love as a free gift to everyone and that includes you and me. Once that love is given it can and will never, ever, be taken back. You are just finding it too difficult believing that it applies even to you but it does. Jesus might not be physically present with you in the same way that he was with his disciples 2,000 years ago but, perhaps, even better than that he dwells in your heart, he is part of you, closer to you than you can ever imagine; you are precious to him and he whispers gently to you wherever you go, whatever you do and however you feel, *'This is my commandment love one another as I have loved you.'* (John 15:12)

The Gift of Peace

'Peace I give to you, my own peace I give you, a peace the world cannot give, this is my gift to you.' **(John 14:27)**

Many people today live fractured and angry lives. Life is hectic. Life is demanding. Life is challenging. People feel that they have no time and they have no patience. Everyone is expected to multi-task and be good at everything. If something needs to be done then it must be done now! More than ever before people are suffering from mental illness and are finding it difficult to cope just with the demands of living. Social media exacerbates this by suggesting that we all need to be *'liked'* and that if we are not then there must be something wrong with us. Self-image dominates, we need to dress, shop and look in a certain way that matches up to other people's expectations of us. Everybody wants to or it seems has to be, famous. We live in a celebrity culture. The pressures on people are enormous but what happens if we can't afford it? What happens when we end up in debt? What happens if we cannot please other people, failing to live up to their expectations and end up drowning in our own misery as perceived failures? What happens then? What happens if we can't get a job let alone keep one and what happens if our whole life collapses around us?

God in Christ comes to us and says, *'Peace I give to you, my own peace I give you.'* (John 14:27) Let us note straight away that this is Jesus's own peace and it is *'a peace the world cannot give.'* (John14: 27) In other words it comes uniquely to us from God himself and cannot be found anywhere else. How many of us spend much of our time, perhaps persuaded by the world, believing that the answers to all of our problems can only be found outside of ourselves? In fact that is why the marketing industry exists to convince us that happiness can only be found in the externals of life. In direct contradiction to this Jesus says that the true answers to life's problems can only be found in God. Only in him can we find true contentment. Only in him can we find true peace. Only in him can we ever begin to understand who and what we really are. But you might be tempted to say my problems are too big and too deep I just cannot see a way out! That might be true but you have to start somewhere.

So why not begin with the words of Jesus? No matter who you are or what you are going through Jesus says these words, *'Peace I give to you, my own peace I give you, a peace the world cannot give.'* This peace is planted deep within your own heart all you have to do is reach for it. It has, in fact, always been there, it is just that life has taught us to lock it away and keep it at arms- length, at a safe distance. But the truth is that God is closer to us than we could ever imagine, all we have to do is learn to let go and place our trust in him. Then we will find *'a peace the world cannot give'* and see it for what it really is, *'my gift to you.'*

The Gift of the Holy Spirit

'I have said these things to you while still with you; but the Advocate, the Holy Spirit, whom the Father will send in my name, will teach you everything and remind you of all I have said to you.' (John 14: 25-26)

Many people in life, today, are lonely, examples might include the elderly and the house bound, those in hospital or a hospice, the bereaved, the retired, the unemployed, the homeless and those in prison. However, at the same time we must not forget children who might be bullied or stigmatized on social media and the famous for whom publicity and wealth can often result in isolation. It is, perhaps, surprising that in our increasing technological world where communication can be instantaneous and where we can travel from one side of the world to the other with relative ease people are lonelier now than ever. It is not uncommon for next-door neighbours never to meet or speak to each other or for people just to accept that living on the streets is a natural part of life in the modern world. It feels to many then, that people have turned their backs on each other almost as if they have glued themselves, for attention, to their mobile telephones or other such electronic devices, shutting the rest of the world out. If this is the case then are we afraid to look up, for fear of waking up to the reality that it feels like nobody cares anymore? It is often said you can be lonely in a crowded room, so I come back to you; *'are you lonely?'* Think about it, after all why are you taking the time to read this chapter? The first step is to be absolutely honest with yourself and just ask the question, *'Am I lonely?'* There you've done it, good for you. The next question is, *'Why am I lonely?'* Then we can move on to the next question, *'What can I do about it?'* and that's exactly where God comes in.

Jesus comes and says to each and every single one of us, *'The Holy Spirit, whom the Father will send in my name,'* will be with you, not just now but for all time. What is this Holy Spirit? Nothing less than God himself, the third person of the Holy Trinity; the one God who exists as Father, Son and Holy Spirit. This is the presence of God himself that Jesus promised, as his gift to us, which flows out of His relationship with the Father. It is the same Holy Spirit that Jesus breathed onto his disciples, *'after saying this he breathed on them and said: receive the Holy Spirit.'* (John 20:22) And the same Holy Spirit that was poured out again at Pentecost, *'They were all filled with the Holy Spirit.'* (Acts 2: 4-5) It is therefore through the Holy Spirit that Jesus keeps a remarkable promise, *'And know that I am with you always; yes to the end of time.'* (Matthew 28: 20) In truth therefore none of us is ever really alone. Wherever we go and whatever we do God through His Holy Spirit is always with us or putting it another way, he is always present and never absent. All we need to do is reach deep within ourselves and recognise something that has been there all along, God, waiting for us but not forcing us. The moment we recognise that, something happens - transformation, by and through God's Grace, the Holy Spirit. All of a sudden we realise that we are truly free and that is when God takes us by the hand and leads us to freedom out of the prison of our own loneliness. Finally, if we take the time to look and I mean really look deep within our own hearts, there will be, ultimately, recognition of Jesus, who is the one holding us by the hand because his wounds will be clear to see, for they are the wounds of the **Crucified God.**

CHAPTER ELEVEN

'In very simple language can you explain a Gospel to me?'

'The beginning of the Gospel (good news) about Jesus Christ, the Son of God' (Mark 1:1)

The word Gospel comes from a Greek word, the original language of the New Testament, and it means *'Good News.'* Our task in this chapter will be to try and explain what this means using the shortest Gospel, that of Saint Mark. In the Roman Catholic and Anglican Churches there is what is known as the lectionary cycle, which means that over the course of three years each of the synoptic Gospels are read out, in small sections, Sunday by Sunday. These are the Gospels of Matthew – Year A, Mark – Year B and finally Luke in Year C. John, the fourth Gospel, is very different in form and style to the first three and is often inserted into each of the three year cycles at certain times of the liturgical year such as Advent, Lent and Easter. To avoid confusion the word synoptic as applied to Matthew, Mark and Luke reflects the fact that they are very similar in style, form, order and content. However, for the purposes of this chapter we shall focus our attention exclusively on Mark. At the same time, I have not forgotten the original question and I will keep my analysis as simple as possible, whilst at the same time emphasizing its primary intention, which is to offer '*Good News'* to the human race.

The difficulty with hearing the Gospel read in church each Sunday though is that the passages are read in isolation from each other and it is hard for those present to see, know and understand just how the whole Gospel fits together and whether the author has one coherent message, called by scholars a theology or an understanding of God. In very simple terms the author of each Gospel wants to offer the truth that Jesus is the Son of God and how in and through his life, death and resurrection, this is *'Good News'* for the human race. What follows now is a simple framework by which the reader might like to revisit this wonderful piece of sacred scripture, the word of God, and, perhaps, begin to see it in a new light.

'This Is the Gospel, Good News, of Jesus Christ, Son of God.' (Mark 1:1)

Mark begins then with the *'Good News'* (Gospel) that a new divine action has begun to deliver God's people; this is announced by John the Baptist who fulfils the prophecy of Isaiah, 40:3, *'A voice of one calling: "In the wilderness prepare the way for the Lord.'* Then just after this as Jesus is baptized a voice from heaven echoes Psalm 2:7 in revealing that Jesus is the Son of God, *'You are my Son; today I have become your Father.'* To bring about the Kingdom of God Jesus has both the power and authority to teach and perform acts beyond human understanding and comprehension. Yet at the same time he is both tested and opposed by Satan or demons that appear to have some control over the world already. The healings of Jesus, the feeding of the hungry, the calming of the storm and the forgiving of sins all reveal that, in Christ, evil is being defeated. However, time and time again the demons oppose and resist the coming of God's Kingdom and the threat that it offers to them. At the same time Jesus also faces opposition from those who reject his teaching, who denounce him and challenge his authority to act in this way. More often than not this is seen in the attitude of the Pharisees and Scribes, the religious leaders of the day. Indeed such opposition can also be seen in those closest to Jesus who time and time again fail to understand his teaching and who, therefore, he really is. This is because their understanding of kingship and leadership does not correspond to that of Jesus. Moreover what they appeared to be looking for was a king who, in power and triumph, would literally lord it over others and establish a kingdom on earth. This of course corresponds to the values of the world. Jesus, on the other hand teaches that the values of God are, in fact, the very opposite of this. For him those who have no power at all are the ones who, by their very nature, are more open to the kingdom of God and its coming. Indeed there is nothing more effective than suffering to make a person recognise their deep need for God. These are just some of the themes, which run through the first half of Mark's Gospel. Yet by the time we reach the mid-way point of chapter eight it becomes abundantly clear that Jesus is not, in fact, succeeding in his mission. Few, save the demons, fail to recognise who Jesus really is and even those that do, namely Peter (8: 27-30), are unable to truly comprehend what this means. (Mark 8: 31-33)

Chapter eight of Mark's Gospel now becomes a watershed in our understanding of the Good News it is proclaiming; for Jesus makes it clear that he himself will have to suffer and die. Once again his disciples fail to understand this, just as they will fail when he is arrested. Jesus is abandoned at the time of his passion and condemned unjustly by the chief priest and the Roman governor, as well as being mocked by the religious leaders. When he cries out from the cross, even God appears not to hear him. This abandonment and suffering is vital to our understanding of Jesus and the nature of God. It was something that the disciples and closet followers of Jesus consistently failed to understand. The teaching, parables and miracles failed to inspire faith and belief in a God whose very nature and being were nothing less than opposite to that which the world expected. Therefore God would have to show them himself what his true nature was like and that would include the suffering and death of his own Son. Thus at the very moment when Jesus appears to experience total abandonment God vindicates him by showing what Jesus had said all along was, in fact, true. Jesus is raised from the dead and his disciples will see him again where it all began, in Galilee. The very place where he called them to be his disciples, where they followed him for the first time, where they heard the parables and saw the miracles but failed to understand. Now Jesus calls them to follow him again only this time they will begin to see, learn and understand the real meaning of suffering and the nature of God.

If you have enjoyed reading this somewhat simplified introduction to a Gospel, which is what you, the reader, in fact, asked for, why not go back and read Mark again, you might just be surprised at what you find there! For example, about one third of Mark's Gospel focuses on what is called the passion, the death of Jesus, why do you think this is? Equally Mark seems to spend a significant time in his Gospel, the second half in fact, emphasizing the suffering of Jesus. Indeed, Jesus predicts his own passion and death no less than three times in Mark (Mark 8-10). Again why do you think this is? Think about it, why does Mark place so much emphasis on the suffering of Jesus? Later in this book you will find a whole chapter on this very issue, see if you can develop you own thoughts on it first before reading it and whether the conclusions it draws correspond with your own. I will, however, give you one hint and one hint only and it is another question, 'Why do you think I have called this book *'Only in the Crucified God?'* Also Jesus constantly tells those who he heals not to tell anyone else. It is as if he wants to keep his true identity a secret, again can you think why this might be the case? Now if you are really interested and want to know more look up and read Mark chapter 16. It is Mark's account of the resurrection, when Jesus rises from the dead; *'On entering the tomb, they saw a young man, dressed in white and were stunned.'* (Mark 16: 5-7) The young man instructs them to, *'Go and tell his disciples and Peter,'* (Mark 16: 7) what they have seen. However, Mark goes on to tell us, *'the women emerged from the tomb and fled, overcome with trembling and amazement. They said nothing to anyone, for they were afraid.'* (Mark 16: 8) Now, once again, why do you think these women, who were followers of Jesus and the first witnesses to the resurrection instead of telling the disciples what they saw, as instructed, simply ran away?

You see the thing about a gospel, remember the word means good news, is that you are not meant to just read it but to experience it. Reading is only part of the process and yet it is also the beginning of something. Mark, for example, according to most scholars was the first Gospel to be written and he says nothing of the birth of Jesus, which surprises many people. So why do you think Mark is silent over Jesus's birth? Then we come to the baptism of Jesus. Why do you think Jesus was baptized? Now none of these questions are answered by Mark himself but each of them invites us to explore the scriptures, to immerse ourselves in them, to experience them and, guided by the grace of the Holy Spirit, seek to deepen our own understanding of what is being said. All of this requires time and yes a little bit of effort but I can assure you it will be well worth it. Throughout this book I constantly make reference to God's word, the Bible, as a way of substantiating any point I am trying to make. Indeed, everything I have written here is underpinned by sacred text. In conclusion, perhaps the best piece of advice I can give you now is to go to Mark yourself and to read it slowly, carefully and prayerfully. Never be afraid to ask, *'What are these words saying to me?'* Equally, never be afraid to say, *'I don't understand this?'* When this happens be brave and confident enough to seek help, after all you have taken the most important step by opening the gospel in the first place.

Now may God's grace and love guide you as you seek to deepen your understanding of him through His Word

('The word was made flesh and lived among us' – John 1:14)

CHAPTER TWELVE

Mark, Suffering and that big question, 'Who do people say I am?'

Jesus and his disciples left for the villages round Caesarea Philippi. On the way he put this question to his disciples, 'Who do people say I am?' And they told him. 'John the Baptist,' they said 'others Elijah; others again one of the prophets.' 'But you,' he asked 'who do you say I am?' Peter spoke up and said to him, 'You are the Christ.' (Mark 8:27-30)

'Then he began to teach them that the Son of Man was destined to suffer grievously, and to be put to death' (Mark 8:31)

Suffering, whether it is physical, emotional, mental or spiritual is part of being human. It is a fundamental part of our nature. Yet most of the time we run away from it, failing to come to terms with it and therefore failing to understand it. In this chapter we will examine the role of suffering in the life of Jesus as portrayed in the Gospel of Mark. Our aim will be to illustrate that suffering is not something that we should run away from replacing it with a romantic, idealized fantasy that the goal of human existence is to 'be' without suffering. However, neither is it something that we should actively seek thereby turning it into some kind of virtue. But suffering is something that we should attempt to understand, to make sense out of because it played such a fundamental role in the life of Jesus and his revelation of the nature of God, as the crucified one.

When Peter replied to Jesus, *'You are the Christ,'* (Mark 8:30). Did he really understand what he was saying or did he still imagine the Messiah as a Davidic, glorified king returned in triumph that would liberate the people of God militarily? It is no coincidence that at this moment, the turning point in Mark's Gospel, that Jesus begins to teach the disciples that he must suffer and die. Peter's response is to rebuke him, showing his complete lack of understanding in a suffering Messiah let alone a *'Crucified God.'* Whilst at the same time Jesus drives home the point that Peter is, in fact, thinking like a man and not God. (Mark 8: 33) Here then we have the first clear insight into Jesus and his revelation of the true nature and being of God. That if he, his ministry and his mission is to be understood, suffering must be seen as a fundamental part of it. As if to drive the message home even further, at this point, Jesus also makes it clear that suffering is also a condition of discipleship. (Mark 8: 34-38)

In our short journey through Mark we will now see how from this point on, in the Gospel, Jesus continues to confront and challenge his disciples, the people and the religious authorities of the day with the true nature of God and the Messiah through suffering. It will become clear that time and time again everyone failed to understand what was being revealed and how in the end only his own suffering, death and resurrection could he make everything clear. In the first half of the Gospel and up to the proclamation of faith by Peter Jesus has been misunderstood and this despite all of his teaching and miracles. From now on the number of miracles rapidly declines as Jesus makes it clear that such signs can only ever be really understood when they are intimately linked to his victory over death through suffering.

It is interesting to note that although the demons recognise who Jesus is (see Mark 1: 34), there is no link at all to their understanding of what this actually means. In other words knowledge by itself is insufficient in comprehending the true nature of Christ. The same can be said for familiarity. His teaching in the synagogue only produces scepticism (Mark 3:21-3, 31-35), the local people remember him as a carpenter and know his family; as a result both his wisdom and miracles cannot be accounted for. This means that there has been little, if any, faith response to his ministry and therefore a total lack of understanding as to his true identity (Mark 6:7). This failure to bring about faith is also extended to his disciples as we have already seen. That is not to say, however, that many people were not enthused by his miracles because they were (Mark 6: 53-56). However, what we are maintaining is that this is not necessarily faith. As we come to the critical chapter eight in Mark the point is made, yet again, about the lack of understanding as to whom Jesus really is. After the second feeding of the multitude (Mark 8: 1-10) the Pharisees still demand a sign from heaven to prove whom Jesus is. His response is to tell them that no such sign on demand will be given to this generation, *'Do you still not understand, still not realize? Are your minds closed? Have you eyes and do not see, ears and do not hear?'* (Mark 8: 17-18). Words such as these to his disciples clearly make the point that even they after seeing the multitudes fed twice still fail to understand who Jesus really is and what this means. The teaching, parables and even the miracles by themselves are not enough. Jesus himself realises this and now his life must take another course. Perhaps the healing of the blind man, Mark 8:22-26, becomes an indicator for us as to what is actually going on, as he only, in fact, comes to sight through stages. With this miracle the first stage of Jesus' ministry is complete, now the disciples will be brought to true faith and a true understanding of who he is and how his life fully reveals the nature of God only through his suffering, death and resurrection.

There comes a point in Mark's Gospel when Jesus, perhaps, appears to admit even to himself that miracles alone will fail to lead the disciples to a true understanding of faith and therefore his identity. That moment occurs in Mark 8: 27-33, when Peter is right in professing that Jesus is **'The Christ,'** but there is no reference to his suffering which in turn for Jesus indicates a profound lack of real understanding. As a result Jesus makes it clear that he must suffer and die with his first prediction of his passion. (Mark 8: 31) As we have already noted Peter rejects this and in so doing Jesus links his understanding of him with that of Satan. As we move on through the Gospel, however, no matter what form miracles take they still fail to inspire a true understanding of who Jesus is. Take the transfiguration (Mark 9:2-8) for example. Here Jesus appears with both Moses and Elijah in all his glory. The disciples do not know what to say other than to offer to build three tabernacles as in Exodus 25-27; 36-38. However, they do take the opportunity to question Jesus about the return of Elijah. Yet, once again, Jesus in reply talks about his own suffering and links Elijah with the now dead John the Baptist. In so doing Jesus appears to be taking the opportunity to point to the potential fate of all those who would bear witness to him. (Mark 9: 1-8) Lack of faith and understanding is taken up by Jesus again when in response to the disciples' inability to drive out a demon he says, *'Faithless generation, how much longer must I be among you?'* (Mark 9: 19) By the time we reach Mark 9:30-32, Jesus makes a second predication about his passion which ends with the statement, *'But they did not understand what he said and were afraid to ask him.'* (Mark 9: 32)

The third passion prophecy is the most detailed of all, as the events Jesus describes are getting closer. By now James and John are ready to ask Jesus about their place in the kingdom of Heaven but Jesus challenges them about imitating the course he must take which is one of suffering. (Mark 10: 32-40) At the same time he also makes it clear that in the kingdom of Heaven service is the only sign of greatness, *'For the Son of man himself came not to be served but to serve, and to give his life as a ransom for many.'* (Mark 10: 45) Once again Jesus is trying to teach the disciples about his true nature and mission but is only met with a failure to understand what this actually means. As Jesus enters Jerusalem on a colt (Zechariah 9: 9) and is proclaimed king in the line of David (Psalm 118:26), this may have been interpreted as a great honour but, once again, shows a complete and total lack of understanding about Jesus and his true being.

As we enter the garden of Gethsemane (Mark 14:26-52) we finally come to the central suffering element of the whole Gospel. Jesus predicts that the disciples will abandon him and that Peter will reject him. Mark is setting a tragic tone of loneliness, isolation and suffering; the fruition of everything that Jesus has said about himself. More than any other Gospel, in Mark, there is a feeling of total abandonment and failure as the drama unfolds. Jesus will now face everything alone. He is condemned by the Sanhedrin and mocked, while outside Peter denies him. During the Roman trial he is handed over to be crucified by Pilate and once again mocked. The continued theme of mocking only serves to remind the reader that everyone fails to recognise who Jesus is. After all despite everything Jesus had taught his disciples about his fate how was such a thing possible for, *'The Christ?'* (Mark 8: 30)

Jesus would literally have to show them if they were to understand. Thus from the ninth hour three groups of people were to mock him on the cross; those who passed by, the chief priests and the men who were crucified with him. Once again this illustrates a complete lack of understanding in a *'Crucified God.'* Mark actually began his passion account with the prayer of Jesus, *'Abba, Father ...... take this cup away from me ....* '(Mark 14: 36) Here we should take note of the very intimate name Jesus uses for his Father, Abba, an Aramaic word, which suggests a familiar and therefore informal family relationship. Now on the cross and speaking for the first and only time Jesus cries out, *'My God, my God, why have you forsaken me?'* (Mark 15: 34) At this point Mark drops the word Abba and replaces it with God. Here, perhaps, we see the full revelation of Jesus Christ, the Son of God, in pain and suffering for all humanity to look upon for all time. No longer would Jesus just teach about the true nature and being of God now he would fully reveal it through suffering. This is what the disciples and all who would follow him must understand. Thus in full communion with God his Father and with the whole human race Jesus actually feels forsaken, abandoned and alone and as a result cannot use the intimate family term *'Abba,'* instead he is reduced to using an address common to all human beings, *'My God,'* yet still there appears to be no answer, only silence, before Jesus eventually dies. How utterly pointless it must have all seemed to the disciples. Jesus the one they had left everything to follow had suffered and died just as he said he would but to them none of it had any meaning, none of it made any sense, how could it?

What comes next is equally astounding. Early on the third day after his burial three women, expecting to find a corpse, make their way to the tomb to anoint the body of Jesus. However, to their astonishment the tomb is, in fact, empty. They encounter a young man who informs them that, *'He has been raised. He is not here. See the place where they laid him. But go and tell his disciples and Peter.'* (Mark 16: 7) Yet the women proceed to disobey the young man's command to go and tell the disciples and Peter what they have seen and heard. Instead they, in effect, run away out of fear and say nothing to anyone. However, we should not be surprised by this in that Mark's theology has been consistent throughout his Gospel that even a proclamation of the resurrection does not by itself produce faith without those who hear it experiencing a personal encounter with suffering.

This in effect is where our journey began and will also end. The women fled in fear from the tomb just as we are tempted to run away, in fear and through a lack of understanding, from suffering. Jesus bids us to stay and trust him. Perhaps for this reason when we revisit Mark's Gospel we begin to see things a little differently in that those who are suffering are very often those who are more open to the Good News. Suffering is by its very nature part of our universal human condition. Yet it is strange that the more we refuse to understand it the less open to God we become. Is it any wonder that those who are literally stripped of everything, therefore, are very often those who are more open to God? Is it because in a suffering and *'Crucified God,'* we also see ourselves? Or is it because all suffering, no matter what form it takes is, in effect, nothing less than a participation in the suffering of the *'Crucified God?*

CHAPTER THIRTEEN

'God where were you, when I needed you most?'

'My God, my God why have you deserted me?' (Mark 15:34)

A reflection on the passion

'I stand at the foot of your cross and I know how you feel Lord. I look for you and cannot find you. I cry out to you but there is only silence. What am I supposed to do? Where am I supposed to look? How can I know you? How can I understand you? How can I be what you want me to be? How can I serve you? I long for the nearness of your presence. I desire with every part of my being to know that you are with me, beside me, in me, for me, even part of me. And yet, there is nothing. So what do I do now Lord, go on waiting? Go on suffering, feeling your absence whilst at the same time dying of my own loneliness. Lord I need to see you! Am I blind? Is it I? What do I do now, I beg you; answer me!'

As Jesus cries out from the cross, *'My God, my God why have you deserted me?'* (Mark 15:34) There is an immediate response from the Father to his Son in the form of the torn veil in the Temple. This event is described in all three Synoptic Gospels, though each author describes it from their own unique point of view. Scholars have for a long time debated the significance of the torn veil at two levels. Firstly, we have the argument over whether the veil refers to the one that separated the outer court from the sanctuary or the inner veil that led to the Holy of Holies, in the Jerusalem Temple. It seems highly unlikely, however, that any of the Gospel writers or even their readers would have had the specialized knowledge needed to understand the difference between the two veils or the symbolism involved.

However, what is more interesting and relevant is the debate over whether the tearing of the Temple Veil is meant to symbolise or indeed reveal God the Father's intention, to abandon the Temple as the place of his presence, with his people, and the main focus of worship for the Jews. Or is it meant to symbolise the opening of a once-closed sacred place of worship to a new group of people; namely the Gentiles, those who were not Jews? If we focus our attention on Mark's Gospel for a moment, we can attempt to get to the bottom of this argument and in so doing begin to understand the main purpose of divine revelation here. Mark tells us that, *'The veil of the Temple was torn in two from top to bottom.'* (Mark 15:38) This suggests a violent ripping not dissimilar to the high priest's tearing of his garment earlier in the Gospel when Jesus was on trial and a judgement was being made about him. Here we can begin to see Mark working out his theology. Reflecting back on the trial of Jesus the tearing of the veil would appear to be nothing less than the fulfilment of the words of Jesus, *'I am going to destroy this Temple made by human hands.'* (Mark 14: 58) As a result when the Temple veil is torn in two, from top to bottom, it is in effect being symbolically destroyed and therefore not being opened to others, even Gentiles. However, the new Temple to which outsiders will be welcomed is not one built by human hands but will be Jesus Christ himself.

As if to prove this point beyond doubt Mark follows the event with the proclamation of faith by a Roman Centurion, an outsider – a Gentile; with the words; *'In truth this man was a Son of God.'* (15:39) For Mark this also echoes the trial of Jesus when he was challenged to declare whether he was, *'The Messiah, the son of the Blessed One.'* (Mark 14: 61) When Jesus answers by saying, *'I am,'* (Mark 14:61*)* he is mocked as a false prophet. Yet now his prophecy and therefore his earlier words, for Mark, are actually being fulfilled because not only is the Temple, in effect, being destroyed, but for the first time in the whole of the Gospel, Jesus' true identity as God's Son is being recognized and by a Gentile, a non-Jew. Here then we are reaching the high point of Mark's theology, his understanding of God and therefore Jesus's true identity as the *'Crucified God'* – all we need are the eyes of faith to see it clearly. As a result Mark makes it clear that Jesus has been:

- Abandoned by his disciples
- Betrayed by Judas
- Denied by Peter
- Accused of blasphemy by the priests
- Rejected by the crowd in favour of a murderer
- Mocked by the Sanhedrin, the crowds and the Roman Soldiers as he journeyed to the cross
- Crucified and left in terrible agony to die

Finally, at the end of all of this and feeling forsaken even by his Father Jesus lets out a terrible cry coming straight from his heart, *'My God, my God why have you deserted me?'* (Mark 15:34) In this moment of isolation and pain the answer to this agonising cry comes straight from the Father; the Temple veil is torn in two from top to bottom. Jesus is vindicated because God replaces the Temple as the place of worship, with the body of His own Son and this will be born witness to by all people, including Gentiles. The fact that Mark includes Jews in this, is seen by the one Jewish figure who now plays a leading role in what happens next, namely that of Joseph of Arimathea, *'A prominent member of the Sanhedrin.'* (Mark 15:43) Indeed, only Mark amongst the Gospel writers describes this as an act of courage.

For Mark, both the Roman Centurion and Joseph of Arimathea stress his theological outlook on the role of the passion. It is only possible to come to belief and therefore true discipleship through the suffering symbolized by a cross which strips away every human support we could possibly imagine, so that all we are left with is God and, therefore, are totally dependent on him and on him alone. This, in effect, is the very essence of the *'Crucified God.'* He not only suffers for us but suffers with us and it is in the pain and the suffering that we all experience sooner or later that we realise, once again, that all suffering is nothing less than a participation in the suffering of God. This is why an understanding of the *'Crucified God'* is so vitally important because it is only through him that, in the end, everything ultimately finds meaning.

'At last through the blindness of my own life I think I am beginning to understand. What needs to be torn from my own life if I am truly to know and understand God? What needs to be rendered in me from top to

bottom so that I may clearly see that, which has always been there and yet hidden by my own self-centeredness? Lord have I been truly blind all this time or is that I have just been unwilling to see through all the struggles, the pain and the humiliations of my own life? But now as I gaze upon your cross and hear those words, 'My God, my God why have you deserted me?' It's as if I am hearing them for the first time only now they have meaning. Lord I ask you to tear the veil from my own life that I may truly see and know you. I have been blind for so long that I almost became afraid to see but now things are beginning to change. As the veil is torn so falls away my prejudice, my fear, and my inbuilt resistance to your self-sacrificial love for all people. Now I begin to see and recognise you in the poor, the victims of injustice, prejudice and discrimination. You are there in the dispossessed, the voiceless and the broken hearted; the forlorn, those without hope, those who have been stripped of every human dignity. How could I have failed to recognise you Lord? Now everywhere I look you are there. I see you in those crushed by the financial crisis and austerity, in the homeless and the destitute, in the alcoholic, the drug addict, the prostitute and all those rejected by society. How could I have been so stupid?'

When we turn to the Gospel of Matthew we find that, once again, God has not deserted Jesus. However, what we do find here after Jesus cries out, *'My God, my God why have you deserted me?'* (Mathew 27: 46) is something unique to his Gospel. After the veil is torn in two, from top to bottom there is an earthquake, rocks are split, tombs are opened and the dead rise. As with Mark we also find here earlier echoes of the Gospel. Matthew marked the birth of Jesus with a star in the sky, whilst his death is also marked by signs in the heavens, on earth and even under the earth. Once again, as with Mark there is a moment of judgement for the Temple and symbolically God is abandoning it. But equally there is a new beginning or a new opportunity, even new life as the saintly dead of Israel rise and Gentiles are embraced as the children of God as the Roman guard confesses, *'In truth this was a son of God.'* (Matthew 27: 54)

'Lord is this my new opportunity? Are you offering me new life? Is this my chance to be born again? I find myself reflecting Lord on moments when I have, like you been stripped of everything. The death of my parents; nothing comes close to those feelings of utter loss, of total loneliness and isolation, of unbearable devastation. Now I see and I recognise my moments of being stripped of everything and it was then that I truly knew you Lord. But more than that it was also then that you truly knew me, for that was our communion, our oneness. Just as the Father never deserted you so you also never deserted me. Now it's like I have new eyes, or are they but the eyes of faith Lord? For some of your people it seems as if it is always Good Friday their lives are so crushed by the forces of a world beyond their control and influence that I find myself wondering at how they can simply live? Yet at least now I understand that little bit more. They live because of you Lord and this is something that those of us who live sheltered lives fail to understand. That when we are stripped of every human dignity you are there and perhaps we can only ever truly recognise you when this happens because at that moment all we have left to depend on is you, our Crucified God.'

Luke places the tearing of the Temple veil before Jesus' death, (Luke 23:45) and not after it as we have seen in Mark and Matthew. This is because for Luke the crucifixion is all about the forgiveness, compassion and mercy of God. As a result only acts of grace will follow the death of Jesus. Now the Gentile centurion echoes the conclusion of Pilate that this man was innocent; whilst at the same time the Jewish multitude that followed Jesus to Calvary and looked on as he was crucified (Luke 23:27, 31) now repent and return home beating their breasts. Goodness even flows out of the Sanhedrin as Joseph of Arimathea, who did not consent to the crucifixion of Jesus, asks for his body so that it can be buried according to the Jewish custom. For Luke then the tearing of the Temple veil in the context of Jesus's crucifixion becomes the opportunity for God's forgiveness and healing grace to be poured out on all people.

'I think now my journey is complete or at least I can begin it again with renewed hope. I started off blind, not knowing, not understanding only feeling the emptiness and loneliness of those words, 'My God, my God why have you deserted me?' They were my words to, born out of the pain, emptiness and suffering of my own life. Little did I realise what had to be torn from my own eyes that I may see clearly, that I may begin to understand the closeness, no the intimacy that we share Lord. However, it's not just me but all your people especially those from whom everything has been stripped away, for surely they are closest to you, the Crucified God. Then finally, comes your forgiveness flowing out of the cross like a river transforming our broken nature so that it becomes like yours and in that moment we are one, we are transformed by your grace. Now I am invited by you to go out and live this good news so that others might truly see and believe; Christ is risen!'

CHAPTER FOURTEEN

'Does God speak to you?'

'Unless you change and become like little children you will never enter the kingdom of heaven' (Matthew 18:3)

In my ministry I have spent much time working with young people of all ages and in a variety of different contexts. The quote from Jesus, above, can mean many things but to me one of the attributes of being a child is the innocence and straight forwardness of asking questions no adult ever would. Take for example the question, *'Does God speak to you?'* Straight away I ask myself where does this question come from and why is it being asked? Children, especially young children, have certain images in their heads, which tend to be simple, straight to the point and rather matter of fact. *'So here is this guy.'* Oh by the way, it is in fact me taking an assembly for example, talking about God. The child sitting quietly then thinks, *'Where does he get all this stuff about God from, is God actually talking to him and telling him things?'* Hence afterwards, the question just comes straight out, *'Does God speak to you?'* My answer, however, has to be immediate almost giving the impression it has required no thought what so ever and, therefore, is perfectly natural. So my response is, *'Of course God speaks to me, doesn't He speak to everyone?'* Now the child will have this image in his or her head of God speaking to me directly but we know that things are a little more complicated than that. Yet the premise remains that, in fact, God does speak to everyone, it is that we just do not listen.

When I teach or lecture on scripture I always begin by describing the Bible as a conversation between God and humanity. God speaks, we listen, but God also invites us to respond. After all, this is the nature of any true conversation between two parties. Once more though the starting point is our willingness to really listen, whether that is in prayer, through scripture, a talk, lecture, a homily or even in daily life, we have to learn to truly listen. That brings me then to our use of language and with a somewhat leading question, *'When God speaks, what language does he use?'* Here I am not talking about linguistics as defined by their country of origin but in terms of meaning. For example we can all hear words but do we actually really know what they mean? Equally how does language impact on the way in which we actually live our lives? Why is it, that today many people hear for example, the word of God, or hear about God and it has no impact on the way in which they live their lives what so ever? Why is it that people even use *'God based'* language without giving it a second thought? The answer, I believe, lies in what Jesus said to his disciples in his farewell discourse in John's Gospel. Jesus was preparing them for when he had to leave, this is what he said, *'My little children, I shall not be with you much longer. I give you a new commandment: love one another; just as I have loved you, you also must love one another. By this love you have for one another, everyone will know that you are my disciples.'* (John 13:

33-35) Notice here the tenderness of Jesus's words in calling them, *'My little children.'* He knew that they were in their infancy as a community whose task would be to continue with his work and mission, so he gives them something new, a commandment, something which has never been said before, *'Just as I have loved you, you also must love one another.'* In these simple words something new was being created, something that would allow them to participate in the life of God himself, through the same love they were to have for each other. It would be much later that the disciples, guided by the grace of the Holy Spirit would be able to come to a deeper understanding of what Jesus actually meant by these words but this would only come after his death, resurrection and the out-pouring of the Holy Spirit. The Church and humanity is still, essentially, trying to understand the language of God as used by Jesus. It is a language linked critically to action but bound by the love of God as revealed in His Son. The language and the actions together are an invitation to be drawn into the depths of God's love but which in and of themselves also allow us to participate directly in the essence and being of God, who in and through His Son loved us first. We too, though, just like the disciples need to see and hear that love in action. To do that requires that we listen and allow God to draw us deeper and deeper into himself to the point that our lives too, literally overflow with his love.

What follows now is a reflection on God's new creation in Christ, through the use of a new language, born out of a new commandment, *'Just as I have loved you, you also must love one another.'* Here God speaks to us tenderly in both word and deed. The words come from Jesus and are therefore God's words given to us but the language is new. This is because this new language is that which flows from the new commandment of Jesus that we are invited to love one another in the same way that he loves us. However, note the context, which is that of Jesus literally dying for the whole of humanity on the cross. Here both word and deed flow out of each other, they cannot be separated, just as the Father and the Son cannot be separated or divided from the love, which binds them together. It is this love, which overflows from the cross into our lives inviting us to be consumed by it to the point that this self-same sacrificial love becomes our way of life too. This is God's new language, something new, a new creation that only comes about through the life, death and resurrection of His Son. God invites us to participate in this new life, which amazingly already exists, all we have to do is to let go of our old way of living and to realise that we are already fully immersed in His love. This now is how it works and this is the language of the *'Crucified God.'*

GOOD FRIDAY – 'THE CRUCIFIED GOD'

A REFLECTION ON THE LOVE OF GOD AS REVEALED IN THE PASSION OF HIS SON

The cross becomes the new language of God's love

Good Friday sees the beginning of a new language; it comes from the cross and is revealed in and through Christ's sacrifice. It is God's own language and comes into existence at great cost. If we are going to learn how to understand this new language and apply it in our own lives then we need to listen very carefully to the words of Jesus so that we too can live the language of love.

Seven words from the cross – the new language of God's love

1. **'Father forgive them for they don't know what they are doing'**

Forgiveness is seen in the language of love, self-emptying, self-sacrificial love. By surrendering everything to the Father Jesus surrenders everything to us. Such is the new language of love.

2. **'Today you will be with me in paradise'**

The promise of heaven; only to a convicted, condemned and dying criminal. Salvation is offered to the most wretched, the most improbable, and the least likely. Such is the new language of love. Salvation is offered to you and me!

3. **'Woman behold your son. Son behold your mother'**

So speaks the language of love. For it is the language of an intimate embrace. If only we could realise that we are wrapped and enfolded in the loving arms of Christ himself.

4. 'My God my God why have your forsaken me?'

Silence! For a while the language of love can only be found in the silence of the Father and yet love remains.

5. 'I am thirsty'

God thirsts for our love, even as we thirst for his. Yet only the love of God as revealed in Christ Jesus our Lord can ever quench our deepest thirst.

6. 'It is finished'

Can a broken life heal the world? Can love defeat hate? Can hope overcome despair? Can life triumph over death? Such is the language of crucified love.

7. 'Into your hands I commend my spirit'

Christ lets go of his life and trusts in the Father's love. We are invited to let go of our lives and trust in Christ's love for us. Such is the language of love.

For now the sky darkens and our crucified world longs for the light of Easter.

Christ now whispers – *'trust in me and I promise you all will be well.'*

This is the language of love.

Crucified.

But soon to be risen!

Some final thoughts

Few people know or understand just how much they are loved, yet in this new language of God this is the only word he needs to speak. He speaks it constantly through the life of his Son. He never stops speaking that single word, which from the beginning has been all he has to say. In his Son the world saw that word, we were touched by it, heard it, felt it and were fed by it. The world and people, in particular today, appear to be afraid to allow themselves to be loved and yet it is this very love which not only makes us who we really are but it is what and who we were made to be. To allow ourselves to be loved is, at the same time, to be transformed by that self-same love, God; who is in and of himself the source and origin of all love.

'God loved the world so much, that he gave his only Son, so that everyone who believes in him may not be lost but may have eternal life.' (John 3:16)

'Does God speak to you?'

'Of course God speaks to me, doesn't He speak to everyone?'

'What does he say then?'

'I love you.'

CHAPTER FIFTEEN

'How Do You Know God Has Called You?'

'You did not choose me. Rather I chose you,' (John15:16)

When people ask me this question I am never quite sure what kind of answer they are looking for or expecting. I have this tendency to associate the word *'know'* with someone who is looking for certainty, facts, evidence, something they can find believable or rely on. On the other hand there are those, perhaps, who are looking for something with a more mystical foundation, which might be described as miraculous such as the experience Saint Paul had on the road to Damascus when God spoke to him directly. (Acts 9: 1-9) For some then when I begin by telling people that I was, in fact, brought up to believe and have faith, the answer comes across as being rather mundane. It is as if they expect something more spectacular and when this is not forth coming they can appear, in their response, to be a little let down. Yet faith for me was just that, normal or least that is how I would describe it. A way of life that involved prayer, reading the Bible, going to church and helping those in need. Yet if I were asked to choose one word that would sum up everything about how I know I have been called by God to serve him and his people that one word would be *experience*. That is because, for me at least, God has to make sense even when life does not.

To understand this I need to take you back into my own life as a child and help you understand how I found the '*Crucified God*' in the darkness of my own life and its experiences. Did I have a happy life? Well the answer to this question has to be both '*yes*' and '*no*.' At times life was good but thinking back even now there is a danger that the darkness of my own memories might still threaten to overwhelm me. You see my father was an alcoholic and my life was dominated by drink, gambling and arguing. We lived in a back–to-back house in Birmingham, which in winter I remember was always freezing cold. We had one living room heated by a coal fire, a kitchen in which you could literally stretch out and touch both walls with a sink on one side of you and a gas stove on the other. There was one bedroom, above which there was an attic but there was a hole in the roof so the tin bath was used to catch the rainwater as it fell through, making that part of the house uninhabitable though I still remember sleeping in it as a small boy. I also remember going to school in the snow with cardboard in the bottom of my shoes in an attempt to keep my feet dry and wearing pullovers that were so threadbare that my elbows used to poke through. I remember the cupboard being literally empty of food, my Mother having no money in her purse and having to meet my Dad from work so that he could use his wages on a Friday to buy us all fish and chips. I remember the times sitting outside the pub for hours on end waiting for them to empty so that Dad would come out and take us home. I remember walking the streets with my Mother and Sister late into the night too afraid to go home because we did not know what to expect, what to do or where else to go. I remember struggling at school, not wanting to go, being too afraid to leave my Mum at home scared of what might happen without me there. When life was like that there was as a fact very little, if anything, to look forward to.

Now I am not telling you this in order for you to feel sorry for me. This kind of life is, in truth and sadly, a reality for many children, even today, in modern Britain. I so wish that this was not the case but it is. No, the reason I am setting this out here is because these were real experiences of pain, misery and suffering for me. I can remember clearly thinking then, nobody heard our cries for help, nobody came when we needed support because the simple truth for me was nobody actually cared. Remember the key word I chose to describe my sense of being called by God – *experience*. Well where was God then in all of this pain and misery?

Things changed for me when one day the Gideon's visited my school and spoke about the Bible before giving us all copies, to keep, of the New Testament and Psalms, I still, in fact, have mine today. At the time I thought this was great but the final story the man who came to us told struck a chord with me that was to change my life forever. It was about a dying mother who asked her son to make her a promise that he would read some of the New Testament every day for the rest of his life. I remember thinking at the time, *'Perhaps I could do that,'* and then that is exactly what I did. Starting with just a verse each day I made my way through the Gospels and gradually things began, at last, for the first time in my life to make sense. Jesus said, *'**Anyone who wishes to follow me must deny himself, take up his cross and follow me.'** (Matthew 16:24) Who was the one person in my life who made the kind of sacrifices needed, which allowed both my sister and myself to survive? Who got up at the crack of dawn every day and went to work often holding down two cleaning jobs just to make sure food was put on the table? Who stayed up all night making sure that we were safely tucked up in bed yet got up first thing in the morning to make sure the fire was lit and breakfast was prepared? Who took us to school, heard us read and told us stories about the old country? Who went without herself, bought nothing of value to call her own but always made sure we had a birthday and Christmas present? The answer was of course my Mum. Again we come back to that key word of *'experience.'* I now saw in her life two things, firstly that she literally everyday carried her own cross and secondly she did that for no other reason other than pure love. In this *'experience'* I saw Christ and for the first time in my life recognised the face of the **'Crucified God.'** In my Mum's hands I saw the cuts and smelt the grease of the factory, the detergent and disinfectant of the cleaner but also the gentle loving hands of the saviour. It was through my Mum that I learned how to pray and how to love, how to forgive and how to show mercy, how to be compassionate and understanding, how not to judge or seek revenge but to endure. It was through my Mum that I began to understand and appreciate how to find God in the *'experiences'* of life because if he was not to be found there then where was he to be found? Finally, I came to a conclusion that the **'Crucified God,'** the one who himself, was broken, battered and bruised by life was the one who came to me in the darkness through the love of my Mum. Only seeing and believing in a God who did this for me made any kind of sense. It was like my eyes had been opened, I was seeing and experiencing exactly the same things as before but I was interpreting them differently. I had become aware of a truth that had always been there and always would be and suddenly his words, those of the **'Crucified God'** *came alive in my own heart,*

'Come to me, all you who are weary and overburdened, and I will give you rest.' (Matthew 11:28)

'Lord, to whom shall we go? You have the words of eternal life.' (John 6:68)

'I am the light of the world. The one who follows me will never walk in darkness. Rather he will have the light of life.' (John 8:12)

When my Mum died I had these words placed on her headstone,

'The light shines in the darkness, and the darkness has not been able to overcome it.' (John 1:5)

I hope to you, the reader, these words now make some kind of sense as they do so for me, even after all these years. I am writing them down for two reasons. Firstly, to explain where my sense of faith in the **'Crucified God,'** came from and how everything I believe in is based on an *'experience'* of God which came out of the darkness of life. Secondly, I am writing them down in the hope that they might just be of some help to others who have or are experiencing right now the harsh realities of life and are, themselves, asking the question, *'Where is God in all of this?'* However, this awareness or awakening did not take place over night. It took many years for me to make sense of my experiences in the light of faith but eventually a truth dawned and everything changed. Our life, the life that we live now, is nothing less than a participation in the very life of God. When this awareness happens everything changes and in all those dark, negative moments of life you suddenly realise that there in the midst of them stands the **'Crucified God.'** For me, at least, it was the only way to make sense out of any concept of a divine being. Not one who is absent or who observes things from afar but one who suffers with you, who shows you his wounds, who bleeds with you, cries with you but at the same time holds you and assures you that everything will be all right. This was the God I prayed to, this was the God I listened to and eventually, I believe; this was the God who invited me to know him, love him and serve him.

These then were the experiences out of which my sense of vocation and service came, so now that the way has been prepared we can return to the original question, *'How do you know God has called you?'* Here, and for me, the first requirement, I believe, is I had to *know* myself, the one whom God is calling. To explain how this works I am going to use a well-known hymn, which I have returned to, personally, several times in my own journey of faith, to explain and reflect upon the meaning of and responding to God's invitation to know him, love him and serve him.

'Here I Am, Lord'

I, the Lord of sea and sky
I have heard my people cry
All who dwell in dark and sin
My hand will save

I, who made the stars of night
I will make their darkness bright
Who will bear my light to them?
Whom shall I send?

Here I am, Lord. Is it I, Lord?
I have heard you calling in the night
I will go, Lord, if you lead me
I will hold your people in my heart

I, the Lord of snow and rain
I have borne my people's pain
I have wept for love of them
They turn away

I will break their hearts of stone
Give them hearts for love alone
Who will speak my word to them
Whom shall I send?

Here I am, Lord. Is it I, Lord?
I have heard you calling in the night
I will go, Lord, if you lead me
I will hold your people in my heart

I, the Lord of wind and flame
I will tend the poor and lame
I will set a feast for them
My hand will save

Finest bread I will provide
'Til their hearts be satisfied
I will give my life to them
Whom shall I send?

Here I am, Lord. Is it I, Lord?
I have heard you calling in the night
I will go, Lord, if you lead me
I will hold your people in my heart

By

Dan Schutte

The words are based on two passages from the Bible Isaiah 6:8 and 1 Samuel 3. What strikes me about them is that they are full of human weakness and self-doubt. The verses are all about God and, unusually, sung from His point of view. They focus on the theme of transformation whereby darkness becomes light, hearts of stone are to be melted, whilst the poor and lame are to be fed and nourished but there is a problem, who will take this message of hope to the people? At this point the prophet Isaiah says, **'Here I am Lord, send me.'** (Isaiah 6:8-9) This is where the chorus fits in because now it is our turn to respond to God's call, God's invitation, **'Who will speak my word to them, whom shall I send?'** (Isaiah 6:8) I found myself in this situation, listening to God's invitation and responded by saying, *'Here I am Lord,'* I will walk this journey of life with you and for you, I will offer you my life in the service of your people, if that is what you are asking me to do. Yet, at the same time, I knew it was and is more complicated than that because before I could utter those words, *'Here I am Lord,'* I had to truly know who this *'I'* was and indeed am.

The first thing I had to recognise and accept was that you cannot through your own efforts make your way to God. Having a vocation is not about hard work aimed ultimately at possessing something. It is not about domination of any kind, nor is it about the object of a search. Rather the first step is the realisation that you simply have to make yourself available, you just have to make room in your heart for the God who already lives within you. In other words it is about finding the infinity within and placing yourself at the disposal of the God who is closer to you than you could ever know. This for me was the starting point, recognising and seeing the reality of God in the midst of my own life and all its *'experiences.'* I call this self-realisation. However, the process of recognising my true self was still far from complete.

The second thing I found myself doing was accepting then rejecting all those aspects of life that pulled me away from God and acted as distractions. I am going to call them forms of entertainment. It does not matter what they are films, TV, sport, music, social media, the Internet, are a few examples, which though not wrong in and of themselves all encouraged me to forget my true self. If I was ever to truly say, *'Here I am Lord,'* then it was essential for me to pass from the superficiality of life to my real centre of being.

The final thing I knew I had to do was change my attitude towards possessions. My thinking process here was, in fact, quite simple, in so far as I had to appreciate fully that I was not the subject of what I owned, which would make me a slave to them. Quite simply I had to become detached from all things except God. Only at this point could I truly hear those words spoken to me, **'Whom shall I send?'** To hear them I knew I had to be free, free from thinking it was all about me and what I could do, free from all those distractions, which prevented me from recognising who I really am and finally free from all those things in life which would seek to claim me as their own. Only now by knowing my true self could I reply by saying, *'Here I am Lord, send me.'* Once I reached this point I began to understand the true meaning of faith for me, which was an act of obedience through which we learn to surrender our true selves totally to God.

I am a Deacon within the Roman Catholic Church. The word deacon comes from the Greek word diákonos (διάκονος), which means servant and very much echoes the words of Jesus himself,

'For even the Son of Man did not come to be served but to serve and to give his life as a ransom for many.' (Mark 10:45)

'I am in your midst as one who serves.' (Luke 22:27)

There is a most beautiful scene in the Gospel of John where Jesus takes a towel and a basin of water and washes the feet of his disciples,

'Now before the festival of the Passover, Jesus knew that his hour had come to depart from this world and go to the Father. Having loved his own who were in the world, he loved them to the end. The devil had already put it into the heart of Judas son of Simon Iscariot to betray him. And during supper Jesus, knowing that the Father had given all things into his hands, and that he had come from God and was going to God, got up from the table, took off his outer robe, and tied a towel around himself. Then he poured water into a basin and began to wash the disciples' feet and to wipe them with the towel that was tied around him. He came to Simon Peter, who said to him, "Lord, are you going to wash my feet?" Jesus answered, "You do not know now what I am doing, but later you will understand." Peter said to him, "You will never wash my feet." Jesus answered, "Unless I wash you, you have no share with me." Simon Peter said to him, "Lord, not my feet only but also my hands and my head!" Jesus said to him, "One who has bathed does not need to wash, except for the feet, but is entirely clean. And you are clean, though not all of you." For he knew who was to betray him, for this reason he said, "Not all of you are clean."

After he had washed their feet, had put on his robe, and had returned to the table, he said to them, "Do you know what I have done to you? You

call me Teacher and Lord—and you are right, for that is what I am. So if I, your Lord and Teacher, have washed your feet, you also ought to wash one another's feet. For I have set you an example that you also should do as I have done to you. Very truly, I tell you, servants are not greater than their master, nor are messengers greater than the one who sent them. If you know these things, you are blessed if you do them.'
(John 13: 1-17)

The actions of Jesus here are quite remarkable in so far as he assumes the role of a common bond slave, the lowest slave of all within the ancient cultural world at the time. Such slaves were allotted the most menial and degrading tasks and yet here we find, Jesus, the Son of God, washing the feet of his own disciples. Little wonder then that they were both offended and confused by his actions. Despite this Jesus goes on to say, *'I give you a new commandment: love one another. Just as I have loved you, so you should also love one another. This is how everyone will know that you are my disciples: if you love one another.'* (John 13:34-35) The very essence then of following Jesus is serving through love whilst knowing and believing that, *'Without him we can do nothing.'* (John 15:5) My own understanding of God's invitation to serve him and his people derives directly from this and yet I first learned what true service meant from my Mother. You already know the background so I will not repeat myself again but she was the one who got up and went out to work day in and day out for me. She was the one who sacrificed her life so that I could be the person who I am today. She was the one who taught me directly and by example what true service and true love actually meant in action. Finally, she was the one who opened my eyes to what God is really like. And how did Jesus described himself, as a servant.

Service then is the very essence of Christian ministry whatever form it takes, that is why Saint Paul in his letter to the Romans begins it by describing himself as, *'a servant of Christ Jesus.'* (Romans 1:1) Indeed, it is why one of the best ways to describe the Pope, the leader of the Roman Catholic Church is as, *'the servant of the servants of Christ.'* At the same time it is vital to be open and receptive to the invitation to serve, which can only come from *'The Crucified God.'* For he is the one who stands containing within his own body the marks, still, of his crucifixion whilst at the same time being the one who through a life of service and love invites us to simply, *'Come, follow me.'* (Matthew 4:19)

At Saint Mary's College Oscott, the seminary for the Archdiocese of Birmingham where I lecture on a part-time basis, it is not unusual for me to come across some students who, unfairly compare themselves, unfavourably in my opinion, to more academically gifted candidates. When this happens I simply invite them to listen again to the words of Jesus and take them to heart, *'You did not chose me. Rather I chose you* (John15"16)

I hope that now you, the reader, are in a better position to understand how I *'know'* God has called me. It might not be spectacular, at least in the eyes of the world, but it is born out the reality of my own life, where in the midst of darkness and much sadness the *'Crucified God'* came to me, found me and called me. My response quite simply was, *'Here I am Lord, I come to do your will.'* (Psalm 40:7)

'Give me only your love and your grace that is enough for me.'

SAINT IGNATIUS LOYOLA

CHAPTER SIXTEEN

'Who Am I?'

'You created my inmost self, knit me together in my mother's womb. For so many marvels I thank you; a wonder am I, and all your works are wonders. You knew me through and through, my being held no secrets from you, when I was being formed in secret, textured in the depths of the earth.' (Psalm 139: 13-15)

'I have come that you may have life,' (John 10:10)

What a great question this is, *'Who am I?'* But where do you even start to answer a question like this? I'm actually going to start with a story to set the scene and then delve deeply into how God might answer this question for us through the experience of his Son, Jesus.

The Eagle and the Chicken

A man once found an eagle's egg and wasn't quite sure what to do with it. So being well intentioned and passing a farm he popped it into the nest of a chicken and off he went. Sometime later the egg hatched along with several chicks and the young eagle grew up with them.

Throughout the whole of his life the eagle did exactly what his fellow chickens did, thinking, mistakenly, of course that he was just another chicken. So he scratched the ground for worms and insects. He did his best to cluck and clack and he would even thrash his wings and on occasion managed to fly a few feet into the air.

Now years went by and the eagle grew old. Then one day he saw a magnificent bird flying in the air above him in a beautiful, cloudless sky. The bird glided in graceful majesty among the powerful wind currents, with scarcely a beat of its strong golden wings.

Once again the now old eagle looked up in absolute awe, turned to his neighbour and asked, 'who is that?'

'That's the eagle, the king of the birds,' replied his neighbour. 'He belongs to the sky, just as we chickens belong to the earth.' So the eagle lived and died a chicken, for that is what he thought he was. (Author unknown)

Firstly, when you read this story how does it make you feel? Secondly who do you identify with in the story the eagle or the chicken? Thirdly how would you feel if I told you that God's will for all of us is that we are in fact, each and every single one of us, without exception eagles! Now how does that make you feel now? How is it then that we just do not feel like eagles some of the time, let alone all of or even most of the time? That brings us back to the question, *'Who am I?'* At this point it might be helpful to admit that deep down most of us are afraid, perhaps, even to live, let alone be happy and content, which is exactly what God desires for us. So here are few words God has to say to us,

'He will raise you up on eagles wings

bare you on the breath of dawn

make you to shine like the sun

and hold you in the palm of His hand'

(Lyrics by Josh Groban, based on Psalm 91)

In many ways the words of this simple hymn express God's deepest desire for each and every single one of us but that does not mean we have nothing to do. Instead God invites us to respond to our own deepest desires, which, in fact, correspond, with His for us. So where do we begin, the answer as always lies with Jesus.

Jesus – who are you?

'Then Jesus was led by the Spirit into the wilderness to be tempted by the devil. After fasting forty days and forty nights, he was hungry. The tempter came to him and said, "If you are the Son of God, tell these stones to become bread."

Jesus answered, "It is written: 'Human beings shall not live on bread alone, but on every word that comes from the mouth of God.'"

Then the devil took him to the holy city and had him stand on the highest point of the temple. "If you are the Son of God," he said, "throw yourself down. For it is written:

"He will command his angels concerning you,

and they will lift you up in their hands,

so that you will not strike your foot against a stone.¹"

Jesus answered him, "It is also written: 'Do not put the Lord your God to the test.'"

Again, the devil took him to a very high mountain and showed him all the kingdoms of the world and their splendour. "All this I will give you," he said, "if you will bow down and worship me."

Jesus said to him, "Away from me, Satan! For it is written: 'Worship the Lord your God, and serve him only.'"

Then the devil left him, and angels came and attended him.' (Matthew 4: 1-11)

I am going to start with a big question and it is this, '*How would Jesus define himself?*' How would Jesus answer the question, '*Who am I?*' I would tentatively answer this question by suggesting that Jesus would respond by defining himself in relation to his relationship with his Father. For it was this relationship that would be crucial to the success of his ministry and would later help us make sense of his words in John's Gospel, '*I and the Father are one.*' (John 10:30) For this reason and before his earthly ministry actively began Jesus takes himself out into the wilderness to be by himself and alone with His Father. We are told in the above passage from Matthew's Gospel that, '*He fasted for forty days and forty nights, after which he was hungry,*' (Matthew 4: 1-3). At this point Jesus would also have been close to exhaustion and therefore weak. It makes perfect sense, therefore, that this would be the best time to tempt him. How strong, after all is his relationship with his Father? If somehow a wedge could be driven into this relationship Jesus's ministry would have been over before it even began. It is at this point that Matthew tells us that the tester, another name for Satan or the Devil, comes to him and says, '*If you are the Son of God, tell these stones to turn into loaves.*' Firstly, we should note here the sarcastic tone, in which the first temptation is phrased beginning with, '*if.*' In other words, *'you must be hungry surely and as you are the Son of God, why don't you do a miracle like turning those stones into bread, that should be easy for you, shouldn't it?'* How tempting this must have been for Jesus to satisfy his earthly and therefore human desire for food, we all can sympathise with him at this point. But note Jesus's response, '***Human beings live not on bread alone but on every word that comes from the mouth of God.***' In other words Jesus will not be defined by food but only by his relationship with his Father, there are deeper needs to being human other than the necessary requirement to eat physical food.

What about us then and what about that question, '***Who am I?***' Well then do we really define ourselves by the food that we eat? Of course not, that would be silly that is assuming that we have enough to eat in the first place. Jesus seems to suggest in this passage that we have deeper spiritual needs that only God can satisfy and that without them we cannot truly live. God sends His Son into the world that we might know him, experience him and live our lives in him. Therefore, that which is crucial to us has to be Jesus, without him our lives have no meaning or purpose. Listen to the words of Jesus in John's Gospel, '***I have come so that you may have life and have it to the full.***' (John 10:10) Here, in essence, is why Jesus came but there are so many things in life that distract us from him, things we think are important, things we think that we need but which of themselves serve only as barriers between us and him, barriers of our own making. This is what Saint Augustine said, when reflecting on the same issue, '***You have made us for yourself, O Lord and our heart is restless until it rests in you.***' (Confessions Lib 1,1-2,2. 5,5 CSEL 33, 1-5) If then, from a faith perspective, a wedge can be driven between our relationship with Jesus, the question *'Who am I?'* will fail to have any importance or relevance in our lives. So what do we need to do? Well the starting point needs to be to identify all those things in life, which act as barriers between Jesus and us, recognising them for what they really are as nothing less than hindrances to our relationship with God in Christ. Jesus said, *"It is written: 'Human beings shall not live on bread alone, but on every word that comes from the mouth of God.'"* (Matthew 4:4) So what is it in our lives that prevent us from saying this? What are the obstacles, which need to be confronted and dealt with if we are to be truly free? This, in fact, is exactly what Jesus invites us to do with the words, *'Then you will know the truth, and the truth will set you free.'* (John 8:323) The first step of our journey in answering the question, *'Who am I?'* ends with defining ourselves only in terms of our relationship with Jesus Christ, the Son of God.

At this stage it is important to keep in mind that scripture makes the point that it is the Devil who tempts Jesus away from his mission and therefore seeks to disrupt or divide Jesus's relationship with His Father. We too need to keep in mind what keeps us from drawing close to Christ? What seeks to separate us from the love of God revealed in His Son? What prevents us from truly being the person God calls us to be? To answer this we need to allow ourselves to be drawn deeper into the mystery of Jesus's relationship with his Father and reflect on what that means for our relationship with Christ and indeed with ourselves.

The second temptation involves Jesus being taken to the holy city of Jerusalem to the top of the Temple. Once again the temptation starts with the sarcastic refrain, *'If.'* So, *'If you are the Son of God, throw yourself down; for scripture says: He has given His angles orders about you, and they will carry you up in their arms in case you trip over a stone.'*

(Matthew 4: 5-7) The question now becomes will Jesus test His Father? What a huge question that is! However, perhaps it holds an even bigger question for us, *'Does God test us? Is our faith in God deliberately tested by Him?'* What a question that is. At this point though we need to pause and give this question serious consideration because it has profound importance if we are to move forward in our quest to answer the question, *'Who am I?'* What kind of God would ever say, *'I am going to test that person's faith in me by making them or someone they love suffer?'* How would such a God fit in with the God revealed by Jesus Christ as the God of mercy, compassion, forgiveness and love? Would not such a God be cruel, sadistic and callous? Does not such an understanding of God fly in the face of He who became one of us in and through His Son, Jesus? If then God does not put us to the test, should we by comparison do the same with him? Let us face the fact that most of us at some time in our lives have asked God for something and when we have not received exactly what we wanted the result has been to question the existence of God or at the very least the pointlessness of prayer. This is, of course, to put God to the test.

Let us reflect now on the reaction of Jesus to the invitation to throw himself off the Temple and ask His Father to save him. Quoting scripture, just as the Devil did, Jesus says, *'Do not put the Lord your God to the test.'* (Matthew 4: 7) And here we have it, Jesus will not, succumb to this temptation, simply because he does not need to test his relationship with His Father. Jesus knows and believes exactly what his Father's reaction will be and this is something he does not need to test, even at his most weakest and vulnerable point. In his earthly ministry Jesus will reveal the nature and the being of God by telling parables, stories with a deep meaning, which need to be considered and reflected upon over time. Many of them highlight the importance of believing and trusting in God, something referred to as faith, no matter what trials or tribulations people may face. One such parable compares the building of two houses, one with its foundation built on sand, and the other built on rock. When the storms hit both houses the one built on sand collapses, whilst the one built on rock survives. Faith is the bedrock on which Christ invites us to build our lives. If that is so, then we can withstand anything that life throws at us, if it is not then our lives collapse and we flounder.

When Jesus is tempted by the Devil to throw himself off the Temple His relationship with his Father is so strong that He will not be tempted to do so because he already lives His life in such union with his Father that irrespective of what happens to Him that unity cannot ever be broken. So in trying to answer the question, *'Who am I?'* We need to reflect on where do our real securities in life lie? On what foundation do we build our lives? How much of our lives are built on fear and doubt? In whom do we put our faith? Jesus, however, invites us to place all our trust in Him, *'Do not let your hearts be troubled. You trust in God, Trust also in me.'* (John 14:1) Letting go of old securities is never easy but once again Jesus talks about a man who finds treasure hidden in a field. To gain that field he has to sell everything he has to buy that one field. Of course, once again, as so often is the case, the treasure is that of faith, the selling of everything he has is symbolic of letting go of that which once meant security for him. If then we are to answer the question, *'Who am I?'* The answer begins and ends with Jesus. He must be the one in whom we put all our trust. He must be the one in whom we find all our security. He must be the one in whom we find true freedom to be ourselves. He must be the one in whom we learn to let go. And that reminds me of story we have explored together before, I wonder if you can remember where and why?

A man was once jogging in the mountains when a mist descended and he stumbled and fell over the edge of the cliff. As he descended towards certain death somehow he managed to grab hold of a branch and hung suspended in mid-air. Now he was far from a religious man but felt he had nothing to lose so he called out, 'God if you exist save me and I'll do anything you want; believe in you, say my prayers, read the Bible, give to charity, be a better person; you name it and I'll do it!'

'Very well said a voice, in reply.

The man was so surprised he almost let go of the branch.

'God is that you?' he asked.

'Yes, of course it is, who else would it be?' Came the reply.

'Are you going to save me?' the man asked.

'I am,' replied God. 'But you have to do something for me first?'

'Name it,' replied the man, 'and 'I'll do it, anything, anything at all!'

'Then just let go of the branch!' came the reply. (Author unknown)

How does this story make you feel? Do you see the point being made? Faith involves a letting go, trusting in and allowing God to be God and believing that if we do this then everything will be all right. This, in effect, was Jesus's response to the Devil and he invites us in our lives to have the same complete trust and faith in him so that just as he lives in complete union with his Father, so do we through abandoning our lives to him. All we really need to do is to, **'let go.'**

We now arrive at the final temptation, this time Jesus is taken to the top of a high mountain and shown all the kingdoms of the world. In effect the Devil says to him you can have everything and anything you want, all you have to do is, *'Fall at me feet and do me homage.'* (Matthew 4:9) Imagine for a moment someone coming to you and saying, *'you can have anything you want, anything at all and what's more you can have it now!'* I wonder what our response might be. Think about it, fame, wealth, status and financial security all of it could be yours. Would you not be tempted? Would anyone not be tempted? So let us now look at it in a slightly different way. What in life do we value most? What in life is most important, most precious to us? How do we measure their value and importance? Would having everything we could ever wish for or want really ever satisfy our deepest desires? And here is the fundamental issue, what are our deepest desires? What do we really want or need? What would really ever satisfy us, if we were brave enough to be honest with ourselves? In truth most of life for many of us is taken up with distractions aimed at preventing us from asking these questions because they are too close to whom we really are. Returning to Jesus, there is, of course, a price to be paid if Jesus is to receive his reward; He must do homage to the Devil, or in other words bow down and worship him. Once again Jesus quotes scripture as his response, *'The Lord your God is the one to whom you must do homage, him alone you must serve.'* For Jesus then His Father comes first and the Devil fails to separate them, to drive a wedge between their relationship and so break their union. As a result the Devil leaves and Jesus can now begin his ministry, a ministry, which will only succeed because, *'I and the Father are one.'* (John 10:30)

In the same way Jesus invites us to place all our hope, trust and faith in him. That is the bedrock upon which we are invited to build our lives. If we can try to do that then we begin to discover who we really are. Jesus had no identity outside his relationship with His Father everything he said and did was totally dependent on that conviction and therefore truth. The

Devil knew that and sort to destroy it from the outset. If we study Jesus's life carefully we will discover that throughout his ministry he encountered opposition, persecution, denial, betrayal, cruelty and brutality. What sustained him, however, throughout all of this was his relationship with his Father, which, in essence, was crucial to everything. We too do not find life easy, none of us do, even those of us who have faith. So the question, *'Who am I?'* comes back to us and our relationship with God in Christ is crucial to answering it. We are more than what we eat, we are more than what we do and we have longings that cannot be satisfied purely by material things. Jesus invites us to Him as, *'The way, the truth and the life.'* John 14:6) He tells us, *'I have come that you may have life,'* (John 10:10) and to do that he tells us, *'you will come to the know the truth and the truth will set you free.'* (John 8:32) God in Christ then sets us free to be who we really are through the life, death and resurrection of His Son. This is why those books in the New Testament are called Gospels because the word Gospel is a Greek word and it means Good News. So the next time you are tempted to ask the question, *'Who am I?'* Let God answer it for you:

'From the first moment of your life I knew you. I knit you together in your mother's womb.' (Psalm 139:13)

'I hold you in the palm of my hand.' (Isaiah 49:16)

'I have called you by your name, you are mine.' (Isaiah 43:1)

'I know every hair on your head.' (Luke 12:7)

I love you more than you could ever know.

When was the last time anyone spoke to you like that?

Finally then and in conclusion we can say, only in Christ is the fullness of life; *'Now live your lives in him, be rooted in him and built upon him, held firm by faith,'* (Colossians 2:6-7) and all will be well.

CHAPTER SEVENTEEN

'How can belief in God help me cope with the strain, pressure and anxiety that life brings?'

'Unload all your burden on to him, since he is concerned about you'

(I Peter 5:7)

'Come to me, all you who labour and are over-burdened and I will give you rest.' (Matthew 11:28)

There are many examples in the Bible where Jesus asks us to come to him when the pressures of life simply get too much. For example, in Matthew's Gospel he says, *'Come to me, all you who labour and are over-burdened and I will give you rest.'* (Matthew 11:28) Jesus also continues, *'Therefore do not worry about tomorrow, for tomorrow will worry about itself. Each day has enough trouble of its own.'* (Matthew 6:34) My final quote specifically refers to the importance of putting our ultimate trust in God rather than being overwhelmed by the problems the world often throws at us, *'Let not your hearts be troubled. Believe in God; believe also in me.'* (John 14:1)

However, for the purposes of answering this question I want to focus our attention on one encounter in the life of Jesus which might help us respond to our problem in a more practical way.

'Now as they went on their way, he entered a certain village, where a woman named Martha welcomed him into her home. She had a sister named Mary, who sat at the Lord's feet and listened to what he was saying. But Martha was distracted by her many tasks; so she came to him and asked, "Lord, do you not care that my sister has left me to do all the work by myself? Tell her then to help me." But the Lord answered her, "Martha, Martha, you are worried and distracted by many things; there is need of only one thing. Mary has chosen the better part, which will not be taken away from her." (Luke 10: 38-42)

In this passage Jesus leaves his disciples to be by himself and enters an unnamed village. He makes his way to the home of two sisters called Martha and Mary who we know he loved very much. They, in fact, have a brother called Lazarus but he is not mentioned in this passage at all. What we are interested in now, in attempting to answer this question, is the reaction of the two sisters to Jesus.

Mary it would seem is the younger of the two and once Jesus enters the house, in her minds-eye, everything has to stop for him. In fact she places herself at the feet of Jesus and all she wants to do is to be near him and listen to what he has to say. In many ways it could be said that Luke is, in fact, describing the ideal disciple. One who places themselves in the presence of the Lord, listening attentively to his every word, taking in everything he has to say whilst at the same time being fed, uplifted and sustained by his teaching. We note, however, that Luke records nothing of what Jesus said in this encounter. Perhaps this is because there is another important point to make which, in fact, creates the framework within which his teaching takes place.

Now let us take the time to reflect on the reaction of Martha to the arrival of Jesus. Here we see something completely different. Ever since Jesus has arrived at the house she has been doing everything she can to make him feel welcome and to attend to his every need. We can imagine that there is this very special guest to be made welcome, perhaps a drink to organise, somewhere to sit, is the house clean and presentable? Then what about something to eat? Is there enough food? The meal itself needs to be prepared and cooked? Is Jesus staying the night? If so where will he sleep? Is anybody else coming? What about them? How long will Jesus be staying for? Luke even describes her as getting stressed and upset about all the work she has had to do so that in the end she eventually breaks under the strain. All the work, the pressure, the worry and the anxiety means that she cannot refrain from saying something any longer, it has all become too much of a burden to carry so she bursts out, *'Lord, do you not care that my sister has left me to do all the work by myself? Tell her then to help me.'* (Luke 10:40)

Now we come to Jesus's answer. Firstly, we should not fail to notice just how affectionate Jesus is in his response by repeating her name slowly and lovingly twice. He can, in fact, see and recognise just how hard she has been working since his arrival at the house and he is concerned about the burden that she has to bear. However, there is one thing that Martha is failing to understand and that is the importance of his followers to listen to him. He will not always be with them and it is vital, therefore, that whilst he is still in their midst that they are not deprived of listening directly to his unique teaching. *'Martha, Martha, you are worried and distracted by many things; there is need of only one thing. Mary has chosen the better part, which will not be taken away from her.'* (Luke 10: 41-42) At the same time Jesus does not undermine the importance of what Martha has been doing. Indeed in many ways they reflect the exact teaching of Jesus, which is to love, serve and welcome others. What Jesus is throwing the spot light on though which is relevant to answering our question is her reaction, under the burden of doing too much work, to be found in the strain, pressure and anxiety she finds herself overwhelmed by. This, in turn, brings us to the core of our question about how can belief in God help us when this happens.

What Jesus does in this encounter is draw our attention to the potential danger within all of us as to what happens when we threaten to be overwhelmed either by having too much to do or by the conflict that inner turmoil can often bring. In this situation we can clearly identify two competing claims on the sisters' lives, which also shed light on our Christian discipleship today. The first is the call to serve and love others in a practical sense, or in other words to live a life of active service in the world. The second is that calling to be still and listen to Jesus. The two cannot be incompatible with each other and this is the exact point that Jesus is, in fact, making. If we work to excess something happens within us very often without us realising it. The resultant strain, pressure and anxiety have the effect of stifling, then crushing the spirit within each and every single one of us. This spirit is, of course, nothing less than the presence of God within us. This spirit craves love and peace, which only

God through his grace can provide. Instead what happens when we work to excess is a spreading of uneasiness, the rising of the pressure, resulting in increased strain and anxiety. In the end there is no place for the love and peace we crave so much and something gives, something explodes and our lives can literally fall apart.

As the solution to this Jesus offers Martha and all of us a way out and the answer is to be found in him. Time needs to be spent with him, listening to his word, finding nourishment in his Gospel. Jesus invites us to feed from his spirit and his peace so that our lives may be balanced by his love. If we can do this then, once again, our lives will be transformed by his grace, so that what we do in our daily tasks, whatever they may be, reflect something of the spirit, the life and the love of God.

As we come to the end of this reflection our conclusion has to be that we do not live to work. However, work very often is a necessary part of who we are but we must never forget that we are made in the image of God and loved deeply and intimately by him. So whether we work or not Jesus invites us to live balanced lives. Only by placing ourselves in his presence, by listening attentively to his teaching and his word, only by knowing and believing that we are loved and cherished by him more than we could ever imagine can the spirit grow within us to the point that we too can reflect something of the nature of his being. When that happens we suddenly realise that we can share everything with him even the strain, pressure and anxiety of life and he will shoulder that burden with us gladly because he is the *'Crucified God.'*

'COME TO ME, ALL YOU WHO LABOUR AND ARE OVER-BURDENED AND I WILL GIVE YOU REST.' (MATTHEW 11:28)

CHAPTER EIGHTEEN

'I'm frightened of dying, death and purgatory – can you help me please?'

'Do not be afraid.' (Matthew 28:10)

One day, as I left church, a member of the parish, with a deep sense of personal pain and anguish, asked me the above question. It is, of course, a huge one and although I answered it at the time, I needed to give such a question greater consideration and depth if I was ever going to do it justice. I began; therefore, with my own life experience commending it to prayer and something surprising came to the surface as a result of God's grace. My own Father, as I have already said in an earlier chapter, had lived for much of his life as an alcoholic. He went from job to job only to waste most of his income on alcohol. Very often the rent money for our council house just disappeared, as did the food and utility funds. If any money we had was not thrown away on drink then it would be consumed by gambling mostly on the horses, which accounted for the rest. In addition there would be the times he could not get up in the morning to go to work, the arguments, the cruelty, the bad language and the shear pain and agony which comes from living with a person experiencing a desperate need to drink alcohol on a regular basis; the highs and the lows, the dreams trampled on and the inability either to cope or make sense out of it all. Eventually he died and I preached at his funeral. I felt that the one thing that I had to be, almost above everything else, was honest and I remember vividly saying these words, *'If only he knew then what he knows now.'* After all these years it is time to unpack the meaning of these words of mine and explain as clearly as I can what they mean by answering the above question on dying, death and purgatory. However, as will so often be the case in this book I am, in fact, going to let God in and through His Son Jesus Christ actually answer this question for me but first we have to set the scene.

The God of the Past, Present and Future

'After these things Jesus showed himself again to the disciples by the Sea of Tiberias; and he showed himself in this way. Gathered there together were Simon Peter, Thomas called the Twin, Nathanael of Cana in Galilee, the sons of Zebedee, and two others of his disciples. Simon Peter said to them, "I am going fishing." They said to him, "We will go with you." They went out and got into the boat, but that night they caught nothing.

Just after daybreak, Jesus stood on the beach; but the disciples did not know that it was Jesus. Jesus said to them, "Children, you have no fish, have you?" They answered him, "No." He said to them, "Cast the net to the right side of the boat, and you will find some." So they cast it, and now they were not able to haul it in because there were so many fish. That disciple whom Jesus loved said to Peter, "It is the Lord!"

When Simon Peter heard that it was the Lord, he put on some clothes, for he was naked, and jumped into the sea. But the other disciples came in the boat, dragging the net full of fish, for they were not far from the land, only about a hundred yards off.

When they had gone ashore, they saw a charcoal fire there, with fish on it, and bread. Jesus said to them, "Bring some of the fish that you have just caught." So Simon Peter went aboard and hauled the net ashore, full of large fish, a hundred fifty-three of them; and though there were so many, the net was not torn. Jesus said to them, "Come and have breakfast." Now none of the disciples dared to ask him, "Who are you?" because they knew it was the Lord. Jesus came and took the bread and gave it to them, and did the same with the fish. This was now the third time that Jesus appeared to the disciples after he was raised from the dead.'

Jesus and Peter

'When they had finished breakfast, Jesus said to Simon Peter, "Simon son of John, do you love me more than these?" He said to him, "Yes, Lord; you know that I love you." Jesus said to him, "Feed my lambs." A second time he said to him, "Simon son of John, do you love me?" He said to him, "Yes, Lord; you know that I love you." Jesus said to him, "Tend my sheep." He said to him the third time, "Simon son of John, do you love me?" Peter felt hurt because he said to him the third time, "Do you love me?" And he said to him, "Lord, you know everything; you know that I love you." Jesus said to him, "Feed my sheep. Very truly, I tell you, when you were younger, you used to fasten your own belt and to go wherever you wished. But when you grow old, you will stretch out your hands, and someone else will fasten a belt around you and take you where you do not wish to go." (He said this to indicate the kind of death

by which he would glorify God.) After this he said to him, "Follow me." (John 21:1-19)

This reading from Saint John's gospel, which though directly not about death, certainly opened up my mind and heart to a way of understanding it and its link to purgatory. We begin with Peter who, in his life, made many mistakes, like all of us, but, perhaps, the biggest mistake he made of all, if I can use that word, is that he actually denied ever having known Jesus three times. (Matthew 26: 33-35) This despite having spent up to three years with him as a disciple and having been chosen by him to be the rock on which he would build the Church. (Matthew 16:18) To me we find here a question, one that goes to the heart of the one I am being asked to answer and it is this, *'What is God's reaction to our past mistakes?'* My own Father's for example or, indeed, the person who asked me the original question. In the above passage from John, Jesus takes Peter on a Journey into his past and allows him to be confronted with his errors. It starts with calling him Simon, his original name. In Matthew's Gospel Jesus changes his name from Simon to Peter, which means rock (Matthew16: 18). Now though, many years later and after his death and resurrection, he specifically refers to him as Simon first and with that, I suggest, takes him back in time.

Jesus is on the shore by the side of a charcoal fire and that brings us to that moment in Simon Peter's life when he denied ever having known Jesus three times because at that precise moment, in his past, he had also found himself beside a charcoal fire (Luke 22:55). As if to make the point even further, Simon Peter also reverts back to his old way of life, fishing and just like in John above we are reminded of a time in Simon Peter's past when he had been fishing all night and caught absolutely nothing only for

Jesus to confront him with a miraculous catch of fish. (Luke 5: 1-7) This for me is when the past and the present meet. Jesus in the present takes Peter to his past and confronts him with the mistakes he made there. So when somebody asks me about death and what that means for us beyond the grave I would have to say it does involve being confronted with the mistakes we have made in this life but I will come back to that a little later. For now let us stay with Simon Peter.

Jesus now asks Simon Peter, note the use of the old name, consistently three times, *'Do you love me?* (John 21: 15-17) It cannot be a coincidence that Simon Peter denied ever having known Jesus three times, in the past, only now, in the present, to be asked whether he loved him or not again three times. In fact by the third time of asking Simon Peter is upset and responds by saying, *'Lord, you know everything; you know that I love you.'* (John 21:17) Jesus is here confronting Simon Peter with the mistakes he made in the past so that he can move on in the present but the sole criteria to achieve this is love. Three times the question is asked, *'Do you love me?'* and three times Simon Peter responds with the words, *'You know I love you.'* Love then, it would seem is the key to everything but now Simon Peter has to learn a new lesson that there is a cost to discipleship, one that will bring about eventually his own death, *'Very truly, I tell you, when you were younger, you used to fasten your own belt and to go wherever you wished. But when you grow old, you will stretch out your hands, and someone else will fasten a belt around you and take you where you do not wish to go." (He said this to indicate the kind of death by which he would glorify God.) After this he said to him, "Follow me."* (John 21: 18-19)

Only now there is a difference in so far as Peter lives his life in complete communion with God through his love of Jesus. It is this love that binds them together, it is this love that Peter is charged with offering to God's people, it is this love which allows Peter to recognise and accept his past mistakes and so to be transformed by God's love as revealed in and through His Son. Imagine for one moment how Peter might have felt when he first saw that charcoal fire, what memories must have come flooding back as he looked into the eyes of Jesus and thought, *'I denied ever having known you, three times. You were my friend, I spent three years by your side, I saw the miracles and heard the parables and yet in that moment when you needed me most I failed you. I just like the others ran away and left you in the garden of Gethsemane. I just like the others was nowhere to be seen, when they crucified you, when the crowd shouted out for Barabbas, followed by those words I just can't get out of my head, crucify him, crucify him!'* When Jesus looked up from that charcoal fire into the eyes of Simon Peter what he would have seen there was only love, mercy, compassion and forgiveness; for that is the nature and the being, the very essence of who God is. However, Peter is not let off the hook, instead he is confronted with his past mistakes and accepts responsibility for them, there can be no other way. How terrible he must have felt at that moment. Perhaps he might even have thought, *'If only I knew then what I know now.'* Yet Peter's life is transformed by God's love, the past is reconciled in the present, which opens a door to his future and in so doing reveals God's plan for his role in advancing the Kingdom through a ministry of love. At last then Peter finally gets it, everything now makes sense only in and through the life, death and resurrection of Jesus, which reveals the absolute love of God for him and for all people. This is a reality he will now participate in, a reality he will give the rest of his life to and in the end a reality that will cost him even his own life.

Now when I come back to my own Father, the original question makes sense for me. Everything is about God's love; there is no other reality, which defines who we are. This is about a love that transcends even death going beyond the grave. Purgatory for me is a place where, like Simon Peter, we are confronted with what we have done in life, where we do have to accept responsibility for the mistakes we have made but we do this whilst, at the same time, experiencing God's overwhelming love. This will be like something that we have never experienced before, just like that moment on the shore when Peter looked into the eyes of Jesus and really understood, perhaps for the first time, what he had actually done. At my Father's funeral I went on to put these words into his mouth, *'I had everything all along, it was right there before me, in front of my own eyes I just didn't see it. 'If only I knew then what I know now.'* In the end God's love transforms everything, even death for, **'He is God, not of the dead, but of the living.'** (Mark 12: 27)

We can go back now to the original question *'I'm frightened of dying, death and purgatory – can you help me please?'* Firstly, it is God who helps us by sending His Son into the world but note the words given to us in John's Gospel, **'For God loved the world so much, he gave his only son, so that everyone who believes in him may not perish but may have eternal life.'** (John 3:16) In these words we find expressed God's desire and motivation for every single one of us, that is to say, it is God who comes in search of us, it is God who comes to find us and God does this simply because he loves us. The fullest expression of that love is found in the **'Crucified God,'** which for all time reveals clearly the true extent of that love. Going on from this we are told that God also desires *'eternal life'* for us all, that is to say a life beyond death. However, what we do in this life actually matters and all of us, Simon Peter included, have to take responsibility for it. At this point most of us are afraid but Jesus in Matthew's Gospel after his resurrection from the dead tells us today just as he told the women then, *'Do not be afraid.'* (Matthew 28:10) Purgatory is the place where we are confronted with our past mistakes whilst at the same time being overwhelmed by God's love, then we see them for what they are, we take responsibility for what we did and we are purged by a love beyond anything we could ever imagine. Suddenly we see, know and understand that the **'Crucified God'** never left our side, every moment, every second of our lives he was there holding us gently by the hand and whispering, *'I am with you always; yes, to the end of time.'* (Matthew 28: 20) In life, death and beyond the grave God is, there is no other; He is the ultimate reality of everything. We can know and experience that now through the gift of faith. So the ultimate answer to the question I was originally asked is this, *'Look to the **'Crucified God;'** for he is with you in life, will raise you from death, will gather you to himself and surround you with a love beyond anything you could ever imagine this side of heaven.'*

For this reason when I think of my Father today I find no sense of malice in my heart, no sense of betrayal or resentment but instead something else far more important, faith. A faith in a *'Crucified God'* who, in himself, experienced everything I experience and more. So in that sense there is truly nothing to be afraid of and it is God, in his Son, who assures us of that. In death we, in fact, abandon ourselves to God completely but there will come that moment of realisation, we glimpsed in the life of Simon Peter, when confronted with the mistakes we have all made in life that

God, in fact, never stopped, even for one moment, loving us, we just did not realise it. If we can grasp the truth of this now through faith, then our lives will be transformed by his grace and this is part of the Gospel message, the Good News, Jesus, in fact, came to proclaim, *'The Kingdom of Heaven is within you,'* (Luke 17:21) just wake up!

CHAPTER NINETEEN

'What does it mean to be a father and a Christian?'

'I and the father are one.' (John 10:30)

Some initial thoughts

I have been present at two miracles in my life, the experience of which is hard to put into words. No matter how hard I try the words will always be inadequate but as they are the only tools I have at my disposal I will, at least, make the attempt. The experience I am talking about is the birth of my two sons Thomas now aged twenty-six and James who is twenty-four. I remember vividly to this day the overwhelming sense of joy, privilege and absolute love, which engulfed me. To be present as a new life comes into the world reflecting the love between myself and my wife was deeply moving. To know that somehow this tiny, vulnerable person came to be as a result of our love and union, whilst at the same time containing *'part'* of us was and remains, beyond words. It is and should be part of the absolute mystery that we call God. Yet my feelings, my thoughts and my needs must be articulated if, as a Christian, I am to make sense of this wondrous life-giving event. Indeed this becomes all the more important as our children grow and our relationship with them changes, as it must. I also have a third son called Lance who is adopted and everything I write in this article applies equally to him.

Faith

I have always understood God in terms of relationship. Nowhere is this more apparent than when we look at the relationship, which exists, in and between the persons of the Blessed Trinity. This relationship is one of pure love. This relationship is the one that Jesus came to bear witness to when he said, *'I and the father are one.'* (John 10:30) In the life of Jesus therefore we see reflected the Father, and in the same way the life of Jesus himself is nothing less than a life of pure self-surrendering love. The essence of Jesus's ministry is to open up this relationship to the human race so that all people may share directly in it. Is it not possible to see in this relationship, deep within the Godhead, the origins of our own relationships? The act of union between mother and father, is this not an outpouring of unconditional love? Is not the fruit of this union, the child, not a manifestation of this self-sacrificial love? Is there not union between mother, father and child? Could not the child cry out that *'I and my father are one?'* It is important to understand that parents are co-creators with God when their union produces a child. Also, this act of co-creation is not just a physical bond but also an act of total self-surrender and self-sacrifice born out of pure love. Therefore this act of union also includes and participates in the self-sacrifice of Christ himself who gave his life willingly out of love for the Father and in order that all may know and love

Him.

It is clear from this that God does not will separation. The relationship of love that exists within the Trinity cannot and will not ever be broken. God sends his Son to find us and to bring us back to Him. God wills that we share in his relationship of love within the Trinity. God wills that our relationships reflect, at least in part, the essence of his self-sacrificial love for us. Broken relationships cause pain, whether that be of death – Jesus wept when Lazarus, his good friend, died (John 11:35) or of trial – witness the agony in the garden. (Luke 22:44) If God does not will separation then the pain caused by it cannot be the will of God. Here we mean separation in a negative, life denying sense. The Father's love for the son is total; total self-sacrifice, total self-surrender. The Father cannot deny the Son, just as the Son cannot deny the Father. Can I deny my own flesh and blood? Can my own flesh and blood deny me?

Thus we have established from a Christian point of view the bond of union, which exists between a father and his child. We have also established how this is a reflection of God's love for the world and his Son. However, it is also important to recognise that such overwhelming love brings with it huge risks. Witness the crucifixion. (Matthew 27:32-56) Witness the Father who waits, the Father who gives free will, the Father who is overwhelmingly generous. The parable of the *'Lost Son'* illustrates this perfectly. (Luke 15:11-32) But we need to recognise here that the union, which existed between father and son in this parable, was never broken. Their relationship experienced pain; the inevitable consequence of any relationship but the pain was healed through forgiveness!

The relationship, and I keep on using this word, between a father and his child will always be one of union. If the two are wrongly separated and therefore go against the will of God, the relationship will be incomplete and fractured. When this happens only rejection, suffering and pain can result until healing takes place.

I know that in my life I will never be complete without my children. They are part of me and I am part of them. We are bound together in a union of love. Our love reflects God's love for us as revealed in his Son. We are bound to Christ by virtue of our baptism – an act by God of pure self-sacrificial love. This is a universal truth, that God does not will separation from him but union. Somehow the union between a father and his child reflects the mystery of God's love for all people. How can such a love be denied without dire consequences?

Perhaps in our parishes we need to rediscover an enthusiasm for fatherhood, for surely it is a vocation of the highest order. It is nothing less than a participation in the most Holy and Blessed Trinity, it is a reflection of divine self-sacrificial love, it is a union with our universal and common Father, it is a vocation of co-creation, it is in essence a mission to the human race. Equally it fulfils a deep longing, in the human heart, to be one with God in union with His Son by participating in His love. To deny this is to provoke a cry from deep within the human soul – *'that without you my life is incomplete.'* The Church would do well to encourage, foster and build up such vocations. For the feelings I have expressed here echo in the hearts of all fathers.

CHAPTER TWENTY

'What does it all mean? Is there meaning in everything?'

The Hobbit or 'There and back again,' The Resignation of a Pope, A Year of Faith and Our Call to Discipleship

'Be not afraid.' (Matthew 14:27)

In this chapter and in response to the above question, *'Is there meaning in everything?'* I have chosen an example from the life of the Roman Catholic Church, the resignation of Pope Benedict XVI, linked it to one of my favourite books and asked what does all this mean for our call to discipleship today? What I am trying to do in this chapter is to illustrate with practical examples that there is no sphere of existence from which God is absent. To achieve this I have confronted and therefore challenged myself with an incident, which profoundly shocked the life of many Catholics. *'How could a Pope possibly resign?'* they asked. Of course, this happened as a fact but perhaps, quite rightly, it challenged many believers to reflect on what this meant not only for the church but also for themselves. Being a disciple of Jesus Christ has never been easy. In fact Jesus himself said, *'Anyone who wants to be a follower of mine must renounce himself and take up the cross and follow me. For whoever wants to save life will lose it; but whoever loses life for my sake will find it.'* (Matthew 16: 24-25) Discipleship can, of course, take many forms but it always involves doing something and further to this will always involve a cost. So here we go, see what you think and how it might apply to your life today.

When I was a boy of about ten I read a wonderful book called *'The Hobbit,'* by J. R. R. Tolkien. (1) Set in a fantasy world called Middle Earth it had all the ingredients and characters to excite and thrill a young boy's mind. There were elves, dwarves, goblins, dragons, wolves, wizards, a quest and of course Hobbits. Now if you are not quite sure what a Hobbit actually is then think human, about half the size of a man with pointed ears and big hairy feet and you are about there. Several years later I read it again and discovered that one of the original titles for the book suggested by the author was, *'There and back again,'* and that Tolkien was a Catholic who very often expressed his faith through his written work. At the time I thought little of this but things were to change later as hopefully you will see in this chapter. More recently I watched the film and then all of a sudden things suddenly fell into place and I began to understand, at least, some of the spirituality of the author.

Going back to the book the main character is a Hobbit called *'Bilbo Baggins'* who lives in a picturesque house built into the hillside of a region called 'The Shire.' In simple terms Bilbo is a home loving kind of guy. He loves to sit by the fire, read his books, potter around his garden and eat food – lots of it; and that is the sum total of his life. Then one day a wizard called Gandalf turns up and invites him to go on an adventure, to take a leap of faith and make a journey into the unknown. As you might expect Bilbo refuses, politely, as he does not do adventures, *'thank you very much!'* He would rather stay at home sit by the fire and read his books. However, Gandalf becomes insistent that Bilbo is, in fact, crucial to the quest he has in mind and that without him it cannot take place. Perhaps here we see a clue as to what Tolkien is trying to say about all of us in that sometimes it takes someone else to recognise the potential we all have especially in the light of self-doubt. In the end Bilbo relents, gives in and goes off on his adventure. He takes a step out of his sheltered and cosy existence into the big wide world leaving his home and 'The Shire' behind. Of course nothing will ever be the same again. There are many ups and downs for Bilbo in the adventures, which follow. He is constantly wracked by self-doubt, feelings of unworthiness and an inability to do what is asked of him but in the end he comes good. Eventually he returns home having learnt so much about the world and himself but he will never be the same again.

So what has this got to do with faith, the resignation of a pope and our call to discipleship today? In 2012 Pope Benedict invited the whole Church to rediscover its faith in the God of Jesus Christ at a world, parish and individual level. To do this, perhaps, we were all invited to go on a journey; one that takes us out of ourselves to rediscover what we really believe in because only then can we offer our own gift of faith to the people and communities in which we live. However, the one small problem here is that like Bilbo most of us are afraid. We would rather stay at home, warm by the fire, reading our books than venture out into the big wide world. After all people like me simply do not do things like that - *'I don't do adventures, thank you very much.'* But if that is true what then was the point of a *'Year of Faith in 2012?'* We might just as well stay where we are and carry on as usual, nothing changes but at least we can be comfortable. Then on 28th February 2013 the Pope resigns!

With the resignation of Pope Benedict XVI the Church let alone the papacy stepped out into uncharted waters. We did not know, at the time, what the future held and yet for all those who for so long had felt helpless, voiceless and marginalised there was hope that anything was, in fact, possible. Just like Bilbo afraid and uncertain to cross even the threshold of his own front door yet somehow summoning up the courage to do so not knowing what lay beyond recalls the constant refrain of Pope John Paul II echoing the words of Jesus, *'be not afraid.'* (Matthew 14:27) Thus although the future now appeared to be uncertain and the Church to many may also appeared to have lost its way, *'be not afraid;'* we have been here many times before.

So for help let us go back to where it all began to the shore of the Sea of Galilee and to the call of those first disciples. How secure must they have felt in their lives; the daily routine of being up early and going out onto the lake to fish, the mending of their nets and the bond of mutual trust and respect that must have existed between them. Many of them, of course, were married with wives and children; they knew their lot in life and, perhaps, rested in the security that it was safe and permanent. Just like Bilbo sitting by the fire and reading his books life was predictable and certain; and then along comes Jesus. In Luke notice the resistance to Jesus' invitation to go out again, *'Master,'* Simon replied *'we worked hard all night and caught nothing.'* (Luke 5:5). Or in other words, *'Why should we go out again? It's a complete waste of time.'* Just after this when Simon witnesses a miraculous catch of fish there is further resistance to the call of discipleship when he falls to his knees and says, *'Leave me Lord; I am a sinful man.'* (Luke 5:8) Excuses are something that we all come up with when we feel threatened or challenged and if we give in to them they can prevent us from being the person God calls us to be. It was Bilbo's first reaction to Gandalf, it was Peter's reaction to Jesus, for many it was the faithful's response to the resignation of Pope Benedict and in the same way it can be our reaction to the invitation to respond to a year of faith. But remember whom it is that is issuing the invitation; Jesus himself and what his response to Simon was, *'Do not be afraid.'* (Luke 5:10) Or in other words do not let fear or your own sense of safety and security prevent you from responding positively to the invitation to follow Christ. Only when Bilbo stepped out of his own front door did he really begin to discover who he, in fact, was. To do that he had to leave behind everything up to that point in his life, which he held dear. The road ahead would be long, hard and difficult. He would be wracked with self-doubt and at times find the burden too hard to bare but the faith that Gandalf had in him remained strong and it was this, at least in part, which helped him complete his journey, there and back again. In the same way Jesus expresses his confidence in Simon with these words, *'Do not be afraid; from now on it is men you will catch.'* (Luke 5:10) On hearing these words, which, in the same way, expresses Jesus's faith in them, those first disciples made a life changing and momentous decision; *'Then, bringing their boats back to land they left everything and followed him.'* (Luke 5:11)

I wonder how many times in his life of prayer and reflection and in the lead up to his decision to resign from the Petrine office Pope Benedict took comfort and consolation in the words, *'Do not be afraid;'* words so dear to his great friend Pope John Paul II, words so compelling, comforting and challenging to those first disciples. For their lives just like Bilbo stepping out of his front door would never be the same again. Ahead of them lay a discipleship, which they could never have of dreamed, for their journey would be one which went to the cross and back again. They too would suffer self-doubt, lose heart and even run away but Christ's belief in them never wavered and it was that which in the end enabled them to triumph over their own sense of unworthiness. In the same way the Catholic Church through the resignation of Pope Benedict XVI had stepped over its own threshold and into a new era. What this would involve nobody knew but we can be sure of one thing that Christ has faith in His Church, just as he has in each and every one of us. Was it, therefore, coincidental that the Holy Father chose to resign in the Year of Faith? We were told that it was a decision he had come to after much prayer and that his conscience was clear before God. In other words it was, in itself, an act of faith. In the same way we are all challenged by virtue of our faith to place our lives in trust before God and to ask humbly, *'Lord what would you ask of us? Where would you have us be? What would you have us do? How can we best serve you and bear witness to our faith?'* Sometimes our response to the invitation to follow Christ involves a letting go and this in many ways can be the hardest part of all but in order to discover something new then, very often, we have to leave the old behind. The disciples found this out as they not only left their boats but their whole lives behind and maybe this is something the church had to do to as it came to terms with the first resignation of a pope in 600 years.

Sometimes we can convince ourselves that we are not good enough to respond to the invitation to follow Christ. We have already seen how Simon Peter's initial response to Jesus was to identify his own sinfulness as a barrier to discipleship. In a similar way Saint Paul describes himself as, **'the least of the apostles,'** (1 Corinthians 15:9) not even worthy to be called one. Bilbo also attempted to deflect the invitation by Gandalf to go with him, as a thief, as not being qualified to do so. We are all, at times, tempted to do this but Jesus sees beyond our own sense of insecurity to our true character. After all Peter denies and abandons Jesus and goes on to become the first pope, whilst Paul after persecuting the Church becomes the apostle to the Gentiles. As a part-time lecturer at our diocesan seminary I come across students from a variety of backgrounds, from the strongly academic to those who have not studied since leaving school. The latter are often tempted to respond by saying that in comparison to their more academically qualified colleagues they feel inadequate and are, at times, tempted to give up on their studies. My response to such claims is to quote Jesus himself who said, *'you did not choose me, no, I chose you.'* (John 15:16) And in these words we find the very essence of our faith. Jesus has chosen us to bear witness to him. But to do this we need to step out, very often, into the unknown and to be prepared, perhaps, to do something totally different knowing that it is Jesus himself who has chosen us. Could it not be that the decision of Pope Benedict to resign in many ways leads the way in this process? Very few people saw it coming but there has been a significant number of the faithful who have greeted it with compassion and understanding. Now it is the Catholic Church that steps out and us with it, where we are going, who knows but guided by faith and the grace of the Holy Spirit we can be confident that Christ will never abandon us, *'And know that I am with you always; yes, to the end of time.'* (Matthew 28:20)

In his book 'The Hobbit' Tolkien takes the least likely of characters, Bilbo, in the least likely of circumstances and transforms him into the hero and yet he remains, *'quite a little fellow'* (p276) according to Gandalf. In the same way Jesus stood by the shore of the Sea of Galilee and called what appeared to be a small group of insignificant men and invited them to come with him and through the grace of the Holy Spirit transform the relationship that existed between God and humanity. Their lives would never be the same again. There would be highs and lows, periods of darkness and despair even hopelessness as they stood at the foot of the cross. Yet all the time the Holy Spirit was at work, God's will being worked out through his Son, **'Do not let your hearts be troubled. Trust in God still, and trust in me.'** (John 14:1)

In the year Pope Benedict stood down from the Petrine office God invited us to trust in him and believe, ultimately, that all would be well. We all have our roles to play no matter how insignificant we think we are just like Bilbo Baggins. Tolkien put it like this, *'You don't really suppose, do you, that all your adventures and escapes were managed by mere luck, just for your sole benefit? You are a very fine person, Mr Baggins, and I am very fond of you; but you are only quite a little fellow in a wide world after all.'* (Page 276)

1. The Hobbit J. R. R. Tolkien (Harper Collins Collector's Edition 2012)

CHAPTER TWENTY-ONE

'What do I do now?'

'I am with you always; yes, to the end of time.' (Matthew 28: 29)

If you have made it this far and you have read either some of the book or all of it then, perhaps, it is time for you now to begin to answer questions for yourself. However, one of the first things to remember is that you are not alone. Never be afraid to ask someone for help if you need it and always keep in both your mind and your heart the last words Jesus spoke to his disciples, *'I am with you always; yes, to the end of time.'* (Matthew 28: 29) The other thing I would urge you to do is to treasure your experiences of life the good as well as the bad. I know this might sound strange at first but it is the reason why, in this book, I have allowed myself to be so personal at times. As a result I would ask you never to underestimate your own personal experiences of life. In this respect I believe it is true to say that faith needs experience. Further to this I also believe that it is through our experience that God comes to us and reveals himself to us. To be open to this is an attitude, which in and of its self, facilitates an understanding of our relationship with God.

I now need to take this a little further and deeper. I have already maintained earlier in the book that it is always God who takes the initiative, always God who makes the first move, always God who comes in search of us, to seek and to find us, *'For the Son of Man came to seek and save what was lost.'* (Luke 19: 10) When we are open to this, even as a possibility, then we read the scriptures in a completely different way and the words come alive and touch our hearts. However, we need to combine this with trust which must be unconditional and which will enable us to transcend our very selves. To adopt this attitude I propose is an act of faith or belief but it is unlike any other act we may perform in life because it affects our whole being and personhood. In other words what I am inviting you to consider, as a possibility, in answer to your question, *'What do I do now?'* is to make a life changing decision. And it is this, as an act of free-will, in other words as your own choice, trust God completely, totally and utterly, place your life freely in his hands and abandon yourself to him. To do this is to enter into a new kind of existence and so live a totally different way of life. Now this is huge and I am not pretending it is not and neither should you. You see this involves recognition that your life owes its very origin and existence to God. Indeed there needs to be an acceptance that your whole being, everything you are, comes from him who is the author of all things. The Bible calls this nothing less than a new birth; *'no one can see the kingdom of God without being born from above.'* (John 3:3) and the resultant faith creates a new person, *'so that he might create in himself a single new person,'* (Ephesians 2:15) *'to clothe yourselves with the new self created in God's image.'* (Ephesians 4:24) In this way our lives are transformed by God's grace, by God's love, for in truth he has and always will love us, it is just that we have never realised it before. At this point, therefore, it is appropriate for us to say that our very existence, as a person, has been transformed, *'anyone united to Christ is a new creation.'* (2 Corinthians 5:17)

The invitation from God now is to live a new form of life, to exist, if you like, in a different way than before, *'so that in everything we do we present ourselves as ministers of God.'* (Romans 6:4). Now we see the world with fresh eyes, we relate to each other in a new way and, perhaps, for the first time in our lives we realise what it is like to be truly free, *'then you will know the truth and the truth will set you free.'* (John 8:32) At this point we can say that our hearts have been transformed by God's overwhelming love but something needs to happen next that is vital if we are to live a truly authentic new life. You see this new way of being has to be lived out in our day-to-day lives wherever we may be, whatever we may do and wherever we may go. In other words we have to put into practice what we now believe, what we have now become. If we are ever going to achieve this and you asked me for one piece of advice as to how it might be done it would be, to never stray too far from *'The Crucified God.'*

Living a life of faith – Prayer

Being open to God and being touched by his grace leads to something, which becomes, as we have already said, life changing. I do not know if that is how you, the reader, feels but your own question remains, *'What do I do now?'* My first response to this question is to invite you to pray. We have already explored the process of this earlier when we answered the question, *'Where is God?'* Now, once again, we need to learn to think and act differently. Earlier the point was made that faith involves a letting go of our life by putting our absolute trust in God, which, in turn, leads to a new way of living. Or to put it another way our existence has been transformed. A lawyer once came up to Jesus and asked him, *'Master, what must I do to inherit eternal life?'* In reply Jesus asked him, *'What is written in the Law?'* The young man thought about it and said, *'You must love the Lord your God with all your heart, with all your soul, with all your strength, and with all your mind, and your neighbour as yourself.'* Jesus then said to him, *'You have answered right, do this and life is yours.'* (Luke 10: 25-28) People find it strange when I say that faith actually involves falling in love with God and yet here we have Jesus confirming that this is absolutely true. Prayer then becomes our response to this. Think about it, when you love a person you want to spend as much time with them as possible and as you do so then you find yourself being drawn deeper and deeper into knowing more and more about them. In this way our love grows. The same applies to our relationship with God. Once we recognise that God is, in fact, the very source of our lives it invokes within us a need to respond. Now we both feel and recognise this mysterious presence within us, God; and our only response to this can only be love. This is intimacy of the highest kind. This is what God desires for us. All our defences melt away and we are who we really are with the source of our very being, God. This is prayer and yes we recognise our failures and our inability to save ourselves but at the same time we are completely overwhelmed by his grace and by his love, which is boundless. Such love invites trust, hope and faith as a means to overcome all things. It does not matter how you pray, why you pray or whom you pray for. No, the only thing that really matters is that you abandon everything to God, *'Come to me, all you who labour and are overburdened, and I will give you rest.'* (Matthew 11: 28) If we can adopt such an attitude to God in prayer our lives are transformed, once again, by his grace. Here, in these words of Jesus, we are told to bring everything to him to hold nothing back and to believe that a life of faith needs prayer. This, in turn, helps us to understand and appreciate something, that a life of faith actually needs prayer and that prayer, no matter what form it takes, is, in fact, an expression of faith.

Now as we have said there are many forms of prayer but there is no one-way to pray. There is neither a right way nor a wrong way to spend time in the presence of God; sometimes there is a need just to be. So if you want to pray for other people or for yourself, or for the world then just do it. If you are happy, sad, grateful or just need guidance then express how you feel through prayer. If you are struggling with your faith, feel alone or are on the edge of being overwhelmed by the darkness of life, then simply unburden this by giving it to your heavenly Father, *'who knows even the number of hairs on your head.'* (Luke 12:7) Finally, if you feel the need to say nothing and just allow yourself to be still in the presence of He who loves you more than you could ever know then that is fine too. Remember never expect too much of yourself when you pray and never be too hard on yourself and never make it just about you. However you may feel, God knows it already and come what may whether you are angry, sad or disappointed he will always be there for you. That is the beauty of God. So you ask me having read your book, *'What should I do now?'* and my first answer is pray.

Living a life of faith – Love

There is now only one more thing I have to say but it might just be the most important thing of all. If I were asked to choose just one word to sum up all the other words in this book I would have no hesitation in saying *LOVE*. It is not just me saying this the whole of scripture continuously shouts it out loud. In his letter to the Galatians Saint Paul makes the point that the only thing in life that matters is, *'faith expressed through love.'* (Galatians 5:6) In the first letter of John we find, *'Whoever does not love, does not know God, because God is love.'* (1 John 4:8) Then as if to make the point absolute, once again Saint Paul writes, *'As it is, these remain: faith, hope and love, the three of them; and the greatest of them is love.'* (1 Corinthians 13:13) I could go on but the very reason I called this book, *'Only in the crucified God,'* is because, for me, Jesus hanging on the cross reveals fully and for all time the depth of God's love for all people. Faith now becomes a belief in that absolute love. And only our love, in return, can ever be an appropriate response. We should never forget that Jesus did not die a natural death but a horrible and a cruel one. The cross is something because of its familiarity we are tempted to take for granted and along with it the love of God. This would be a huge mistake. God's love comes at a terrible price but is given willingly so that we might know and understand just how much we mean to him. Of course when we search the scriptures we discover something quite remarkable that God has, in fact, always loved humanity, *'I have loved you with an eternal love.'* (Jeremiah 31:3) For this reason I often describe the Bible as God's love letter to the human race.

However, with the death and resurrection of Jesus something quite remarkable began to take place in so far as humanity actually began to believe that God did, in fact, love us. This flows from the life of Jesus, which the early church now saw through the prism of his death and resurrection and when that happened everything changed. What emerged was a newness in understanding, in seeing Jesus as the revelation of God's love for humanity and what is more he had actually walked this earth. In his letter to Titus Saint Paul expresses it tenderly like this, in Jesus *'the goodness and love of God for humanity appeared.'* (Titus 3:4) I cannot emphasise here enough just how important and how new this expression of belief in God was at the time. That God **LOVED** all people, the whole of humanity without exception. This is what comes to us from the cross and it is so original, so new, so earth shatteringly different that only a revelation from the *'Crucified God'* himself can provide us with an adequate source. Humanity could not possibly have worked this out alone or by itself only faith, touched by crucified love, could have done so. This is what changed everything in those early days of the Christian faith, this is what opened the eyes of those who, up to this point in time, were stumbling blind in the dark yearning for the light. This is what became the Gospel or the Good News and we see it bursting from the pages of our sacred text, *'God so loved the world that he gave his only Son,'* (John 3:16) *'See what love the Father has for us.'* (1 John 3:1) This is what inspired Peter, Paul and all the other apostles to give their very lives to bear witness to the truth and this is what faith invites us to believe today.

When those early Christians looked back at the life of Jesus through his death and resurrection everything was transformed and they could not believe, at least at first, what they found. They discovered something entirely new and it transformed, note how many times I keep on using this word, their entire understanding of God. Firstly, Jesus, as God, reveals the absolute nature of God's love for the human race. Secondly, though humanity had fallen away from God his love remained. The time that Jesus, in his earthly ministry, spent with sinners and outcasts, those rejected, despised and unwanted by the religious leaders of the day, now made perfect sense. The fact that Jesus, innocent though he was, went willingly to his cruel and humiliating death for the sake of all people demonstrates clearly and unambiguously the depth of his love for everyone. Saint Paul sums it up by saying, *'While we were still sinners,*

Christ died for us.' (Romans 5:8)

On discovering this truth those early Christians decided that there could only be one appropriate response, faith through love. It was as if God's love had awakened within them a new way of being human and that was the way of love. Such love then had to be expressed in two ways, firstly love of God because, **'God has poured out his love into our hearts by the Holy Spirit, whom he has given us'** (Romans 5:5) and secondly by love for one another, **'let us love each other, since love comes from God.'** (1John 4:7) Now there is recognition that all love comes from God but such love, through the **'Crucified God'** is, in fact, to be found in powerlessness and yet invites an intimacy with God beyond anything which humanity had ever imagined before. God's love comes to us through the pain and misery of the cross and does nothing less than embrace us and say, **'I have called you by your name, you are mine,'** (Isaiah 43:1) and **'I hold you in the palm of my hand,'** (Isaiah 49:16) I love you more than you could ever know, now share in my life.

So what does this mean for how we live our lives today? It is interesting to note that Jesus only gave one commandment to his disciples, **'love one another in the same way I have loved you.'** (John 15:12-17) He also went on to say, **'By this all people shall know that you are one of my disciples, if you love one another.'** (John 13:33-35) The authentic witness of a disciple of Jesus, therefore, is to love but to love in the same way that he did, as the **'Crucified God.'** These words of Jesus come to us just after he had washed and dried with a towel, the feet of his disciples. The early Christians saw this unparalleled event, God acting as a slave, through his death and resurrection and everything changed. As a result, for them, these actions now made perfect sense and the time Jesus spent with the rejected, despised, unwanted and unloved were all seen as, nothing less, than an expression of God's love.

Of course we still have such people with us today, especially the poor and this has given rise to a new theology or way of understanding God. It is often referred to as a preferential option for the poor and involves a way of experiencing God whilst at the same time participating in his life. This is of course not something new as the prophets often spoke of the need to defend the poor, *'Learn to do right; seek justice. Defend the oppressed. Take up the cause of the fatherless, plead the cause of the widow.'* (Isaiah 58: 6-11)

For the Christian, however, once you define God as love, then all actions of love are, in effect, an expression of God. Saint John put it like this; *'we know we have passed from death to life because we love our brothers.'* (1 John 3:14) Equally Jesus not only spent time with the poor but actually identified himself with them to the point that our response to those in need is actually our response to him; *'Whatever you did for one of the least of these brothers of mine, you did for me, for I was hungry and you gave me something to eat, thirsty and you gave me something to drink, I was a stranger and you made me feel welcome, I was sick and in prison and you came to visit me.'* (Matthew 25: 35-40) At this point I want to make something abundantly clear. The final question in this book is, *'What do I do now?'* We have been exploring how Christians should respond to the poor and all those in need not as a matter of morality or of doing the right thing but as a realisation or a making present of faith. In other words, if you ask me the question, what should I do now as a way of living out my faith? I would reply go and serve those in need, put what you believe into practice and understand that to love and serve others is in fact also to love and serve God.

As I come towards the end of this book I find myself returning to Saint Paul for whom I have a tremendous amount of admiration and respect. As an apostle of Christ his faith was born out of experience a constant theme of this book. He believed in a God who became a slave for the human race, literally emptying himself for us. (Philippians 2: 6-11) He believed in a God who would not allow anything to separate us from him, not even death. (Romans 8: 38-39) He believed in a God who loved and died for us. (Romans 5:8) He believed in a God through whom we become a new creation by virtue of our faith. (2 Corinthians 5:17) As for the *'Crucified God'* Paul was able to say, *'May I never boast of anything except the cross of our Lord Jesus Christ, through which the world is crucified to me and I to the world.'* (Galatians 6:14) Finally, when it comes to the living out of faith, that is to say our call to love like God there can be no better summation than that which is found in his first letter to the Corinthians. Here in chapter thirteen we have a treasure trove of what Christian love actually is, *'Love bears all things, believes all things, hopes all things, endures all things. Love never fails. Love is patient. Love is kind. Love is not envious. Love is never rude and does not seek its own advantage. Finally there are three things, which last: faith, hope and love and the greatest of these is love.'* So when you ask me the question, *'What do I do now?'* Paul has answered it for me and to be honest I cannot do better than that.

However, to finish I have to return to the source of everything, that is to say God and the final word must belong to him. Once again, after Jesus had washed and dried the feet of his disciples he said to them, *'I give you a new commandment: love one another. Just as I have loved you, so you should also love one another. This is how everyone will know you are my disciples if you love one another.'* (John 13: 34-35) When Jesus told the parable of the Good Samaritan as the way of answering the question, *'Who is my neighbour?'* He made it clear that our neighbour is anyone and everyone in need. Then looking up and into the eyes of the lawyer who asked him the question, in the first place, Jesus finishes his answer with these words, which I now offer to you, the reader, as my way of finishing this book, *'Go and do the same yourself.'* (Luke 10: 37)

Some Final Thoughts

**'I call you friends because I have made known to you everything that
I have learnt from my Father' (John 15:15)**

*It is now time for you to write your own story though you may find that in
many ways it has already been written and is, in fact, far from over. You
see something happens when you look at life through the eyes of faith. Take
the early Christians all those centuries ago when the Holy Spirit touched
them for the first time, an awakening within them gradually began to take
place. They looked back at the life of Jesus through his death and
resurrection and saw everything differently and now perhaps, for the very
first time, they actually began to understand what it all meant. In the same
way the Holy Spirit invites us to look at our own lives and to see in our
experiences nothing less than the presence of God. Someone said to me
recently when you write you tend, at least at times, to be a little bit too
personal. I thanked them and thought to myself that is exactly right. I know
at times, even in this book, I have shared with you some of my own*

personal experiences of life but here is the thing, I have learnt that this is what the Holy Spirit has been urging me to do all along. This is because God desires intimacy with us and for us with him. After all in Jesus God actually shares his life with us and surely you cannot get more personal than that. Think of the relationship that existed between Jesus, Mary and Joseph and what do you get? That is right, intimacy. Think of the relationship that exists between Father, Son and Holy Spirit and once again what do you get? Intimacy. I have said it before and I will say it again, God is closer to us than we could ever imagine and what would you call that? Again I would call it intimacy. What would you call it?

Part of the reason for me writing this book was to help people understand the closeness of God to us and our inability to grasp this truth. When we do, that is when everything changes and it is like waking up to the reality of life for the very first time. So I would say look at your life, search your experiences and find God there. It will not be easy it might even be painful at times but eventually something will happen to help you understand that it has, in fact, been God who has come to find you. When that day dawn's life changes, your eyes are opened and you wake up. Now you see everything differently and you suddenly discover that God is everywhere. In every face, in every situation, in every experience, in fact there is nowhere that God is absent from. That is why I have written this book and I hope that now it makes some kind of sense to you, the reader.

Finally then and in conclusion my last words have to be about Jesus because for me, ultimately, everything in this book is about him, the **'Crucified God.'** *In the New Testament many titles are given to Jesus such as Lord, Messiah, Shepherd, Christ and King. However, Jesus himself says something beautiful about our relationship with him in the Gospel of John.*

Talking to his disciples but equally to us he puts it like this, **'I shall no longer call you servants, because a servant does not know his master's business; I call you friends because I have made known to you everything that I have learnt from my Father.'** *(John 15:15) Now imagine that, the* **'Crucified God'** *actually calls us, yes, you and me, his friends. So you tell me can our relationship with God get more personal than that? Jesus, our friend, also invites us, no matter what we face in life, simply to trust him when he says,* **'Do not let your hearts be troubled. You trust in God trust also in me.'** *(John 14:1) In the end, whatever you decide to do now, take these final words of his to heart and keep them close,* **'And look, I am with you always; yes, to the end of time.'** *(Matthew 28: 20)*

If I but call your name

Will you come and follow me
If I but call your name?
Will you go where you don't know
And never be the same?
Will you let my love be shown,
Will you let my name be known,
Will you let my life be grown
In you and you in me?

Will you leave yourself behind
If I but call your name?
Will you care for cruel and kind
And never be the same?
Will you risk the hostile stare
Should your life attract or scare?
Will you let me answer prayer
In you and you in me?

Will you let the blinded see
If I but call your name?
Will you set the prisoners free
And never be the same?
Will you kiss the leper clean,
And do such as this unseen,
And admit to what I mean
In you and you in me?

Will you love the 'you' you hide
If I but call your name?
Will you quell the fear inside
And never be the same?
Will you use the faith you've found
To reshape the world around,

Through my sight and touch and sound
In you and you in me?

Lord, your summons echoes true
When you but call my name.
Let me turn and follow you
And never be the same.
In your company I'll go
Where your love and footsteps show.
Thus I'll move and live and grow
In you and you in me.

Matthew 19:21; Genesis 48:16; 2 Thessalonians 1:12; John 17:23; John
14:20; Job 39:11; Isaiah 10:3;Psalm 146:7;

Copyright:

Thank You

'Love one another, as I have loved you' (John 13:34)

Finally there are so many people I want to thank in the writing of this book. Firstly, anyone who has ever asked me a question which, perhaps unknown to them, has sparked in me the grace of God's Holy Spirit in my response. Then there is the parish, people and school of Our Lady of the Wayside but especially Father Gerardo Fabrizio who have all inspired, supported and encouraged me so much. I would also like to mention the staff and pupils of Bromsgrove School and in particular Jacqui Deval-Reed and Lesley Brookes who not only believed in me but had the vision to recognise that my ministry could contribute much to the life of the community. I have, of course, learnt that this is something which works both ways. Then there is my family starting with my wife Pamela. She has and continues to be a constant source of strength to me believing in me and supporting me when, at times, at least it appeared that no one else did. For all your love and devotion and for putting up with me for so long, a massive heart-felt thank you. Then there are my three sons, Lance, Thomas and James who never stop challenging me and trying to catch me out! Thanks lads, for little did you know that it was God's grace working through you all along. I would also like to thank my sister Kate, who shared many of the experiences with me that I have described in the pages of this book. I hope now that they make a little more sense to you and that you can see that even in the darkest of moments God was, in fact, there all along. Of course I need to thank my Mum who was instrumental to me writing this book. She may never read a single word of it in this life but by the grace of God she has been with me every step of the way. One day I knew that I would have to write her story and in the pages of this book I hope that I have done just that. I would also like to thank Sue and Mike Conway and all the team at ALIVE publishing for believing in me and supporting the first part of this project, 'Born For Us,' dedicated to God in Christ and the advancement of His Kingdom. Then finally there is the reader and by that I mean you. Thank you for taking the time to read some or indeed all of this book and for dipping into your own pocket to pay for it. I hope that in some small way you found it helpful. Finally I have to thank God, without whom I could not have written a single word. To Him be praise and glory now and for evermore.

Deacon Sean Loone

Easter 2020

POSTSCRIPT

I am writing this in the midst of the human disaster surrounding the Coronavirus called, COVID-19. It has attacked all people throughout the world not discriminating on the basis of income, class, colour or creed. It is without mercy and has struck terror into the hearts and minds of millions. This is a fact.

As an author you can imagine that I submit my proposed manuscript to publishers who, I hope, might be willing, for the most part, to show potential interest in a book with a religious theme. Unfortunately I found that most such publishers were only interested in books that would appeal to a very narrow, parish based, readership that would lend itself to potential profit making. Now do not get me wrong I am not that naïve to not recognise that publishers need first and foremost to cover their costs and hope, on top of this, to make a modest profit. However, I was slightly disillusioned by the failure to recognise and appreciate that people other than those with a religious faith might be interested to read such a book as this. In fact this is why I wrote the book in the first place to recognise that God is not limited by religion and that the **'Crucified God'** comes for all people, the whole of humanity, leaving no one out. This is what Jesus said, *'I have other sheep too that do not belong to this fold. I must lead them* *as well, and they will hear my voice. Thus, there will be one flock, one shepherd.'* (John 10:16) Here Jesus makes it clear who he has come for and in the end will die for, everyone! So this brings me back to the readership of this book, it is for everyone, leaving nobody out, which I hope is a reflection of God's will as expressed through His Son.

For me this is a vital role of the mission of the church, to get this message across, that God loves all people, that God comes for all people and that through the life, death and resurrection of the **'Crucified God'** this is made plain for all to see. The Prophet Isaiah expressed it like this; *'I have made you a light to the nations.'* (Isaiah 42:6) This then for me, at least, is part of the role and function of the church, to be inclusive and not exclusive, to include everyone and exclude no one.

On Friday 27th March 2020 Pope Francis gave his Urbi et Orbi, address and blessing, to the whole world in the midst of the Coronavirus. He used a passage from Mark's Gospel when Jesus and his disciples were on a boat in the Sea of Galilee and a violent storm arose. (Mark 4:35-41) The disciples were afraid that they were going to die so they woke Jesus up and he then clamed the storm. Pope Francis drew links between this event described in Mark's Gospel and what is going on in the world right now. The storm represents the Coronavirus, which is attacking, without mercy, the human race and the disciples represent us and when I say us I mean all of us, all human beings that is to say everybody. They and therefore we are afraid and anxious, full of uncertainties about what is going to happen and whether we might live or die. The boat now becomes the whole world to whom the Pope speaks as the Church and he exhorts the people to do one thing as did Jesus to His disciples all those years ago and that is to have faith. In the face of fear and uncertainty God calls us, all of us, to put all our hope, all our trust and all our faith in Him, for faith drives out fear. God therefore, in the words of Pope Francis asks all of us not to be afraid, for God does not leave us at the mercy of the storm but is with us in the midst of it.

My great hope summed up in the pages of this book is that the Church to which I belong will continue to fully realise its call and mission to be a Church for all people, to include everyone and exclude no one, to follow in the footsteps of its master by being the servant of all and by reflecting the loving embrace of the **'Crucified God'** from the cross, whose broken arms enfold each and every single one of us.

Deacon Sean Loone

Easter 2020

ABOUT THE AUTHOR

Sean Loone is a Roman Catholic Deacon working in the Archdiocese of Birmingham. He has spent much of his career teaching in a variety of schools and colleges combining this with lecturing part-time at Saint Mary's College Oscott, the seminary for the Archdiocese. Currently he acts as chaplain and Religious Education advisor to a number of academic establishments including Our Lady of the Wayside, his home parish, where he is also the Catholic Life governor. His academic interests, on which he has published many articles, include Biblical studies and Christology. His most recent publication was a book called, *'Born For Us – A Journey Into the Real Meaning of Christmas.'* He also has extensive pastoral and sacramental experience combining this with a ministry dedicated to proclaiming God's word through both preaching and teaching the scriptures. He is married with three sons and is currently working on a new project, which aims, this time, to explore the real meaning of Easter.

BY THE SAME AUTHOR

'BORN FOR US – A Journey Into the Real Meaning of Christmas'

(Alive Publishing 2019)

CREDITS

Front Cover artwork - Sophie Hobbs

Technical Advisor – Thomas Loone

Constant Support – Pamela Loone

Mentor – James Loone

Critical Advisor – Lance Loone

Finally I need to recognise and give credit to all those people who, over the years, have asked me a question. Sometimes it's a little child in a reception class at school who simply wants to know why? On other occasions it's a struggling teenager trying to make sense out of everything. Then there comes the adult for whom life has become almost too much to endure or the parishioner who simply wants to be reassured that God is still there. Thank you for asking me and for placing your trust in me, it has been a real privilege to be part of your journey. I only hope that in some small way the answers I have tried to give to your questions have been of some help. So finally I would say this, never grow tired or be afraid of asking questions because this is exactly what God invites us to do. You see I believe that all of the answers to all of our questions can only be found in 'The Crucified God.'

May God bless you and all those you love now and always.

Deacon Sean

July 2020

In Loving Memory of

Bridie Philomena Bernadette (Conroy) Loone

Born 1st March 1929

Kilbride

Swinford

Mayo

Eire

Died 24th March 2000

**'The light shines in the darkness and the darkness has not overcome
it'**

(John 1:5)

Printed in Great Britain
by Amazon